A Manual For Wellbeing

ALSO BY BILL DORIGAN
Finding the Midline

LuHen Publications, LLC
300 East Hill Road, Middlesex, VT 05602

Cover and interior design: Laura Smyth, smythtypedesign.com

ISBN 978-0-9893812-2-2
Printed in the United States.

To purchase books in quantity please contact the publisher directly:
info@findingthemidline.com

A Manual For Wellbeing
Using Yoga to Enrich Your Life

Bill Dorigan

LuHen Publications, LLC

Contents

Foreward

I first met Bill Dorigan in the mid-1990's when I was asked to join a team of expert witnesses for a lawsuit he was managing. In those early years of our relationship it was very clear that the man was intense. You will see evidence of this in the ensuing chapters of this book. Over the next two decades we became good friends during which time I noted a distinct change in his demeanor. He was nice. He listened, and he smiled more. Bill, what's up with that? I came to learn that this high-powered attorney, black belt in a couple of martial arts disciplines, fitness fanatic, had added yoga to his exercise routine. More importantly, as he did when practicing law, Bill totally immersed himself in this ancient form of mind-body connection and became deeply involved as a student and ultimately as an accomplished teacher. At the same time, he enrolled in a master's degree program in Human Development focusing on how yoga practices and philosophy can be the ideal vehicle leading to enhanced wellbeing. This book describes his 20 plus year journey of learning, understanding, practicing, and teaching the important elements that lead to wellbeing. It very likely accounted for my now mellow, positive, mindful, and flourishing friend.

A Manual for Wellbeing is an engaging, well researched book that asks if there isn't something more to life than what we are experiencing now. I've asked this question often despite a wonderful, successful family, career accomplishments, a few good friends, and material goods whose luster wears off sooner than expected. What have I been missing? I was intrigued when Bill first told me he was writing this book about wellbeing, authenticity, awareness, and the role that yoga might play in achieving a more meaningful, enriched life. I asked to read it hopeful that I might find information and guidance toward that "something more" that I was missing. I reviewed an advanced draft and found that *A Manual for Wellbeing* is a synthesis of years of expert study on the elements that drive wellbeing: clarity of thinking, positivity, focus, self-understanding, resilience, and meaningfulness. Bill carefully explains and clearly illustrates these principles with examples from his own and others' experiences, often amusing, that have resonated with my own life. A very specific example was the story he related about rock climbing. This was a sport I did regularly for many years with a very good friend. One aspect of this sport, perhaps the major one, is the need for complete focus. Bill refers to this as "engagement," being absorbed in an activity such that we lose track of virtually everything else, complete concentration leading to loss of self in favor of merging with the activity at hand. I don't have a fear of heights, but I'd rather not fall. Getting distracted by thinking about things other than climbing or even negative thinking is dangerous. Finding that nub of rock for smearing a shoe and carefully pushing upward for a more "bombproof" hold requires total concentration, focus, and positive thinking. It took 20 years and this book to bring me to the realization that those experiences were examples of staying engaged, remaining positive, accomplishing more, and sensing more enjoyment. Perhaps this was my entry into the world of what I was missing.

So, then, in the final chapters of *A Manual for Wellbeing*, Bill describes how yoga and its underlying philosophy can provide a vehicle that adds to one's journey toward wellbeing. He refers to yoga's ability to do this as achieving clarity of mind through controlling competing thoughts that may lead us away from what is more meaningful. Bill once again synthesizes research, thoughts, and guidance from many acclaimed psychologists, psychiatrists, neurologists, and yoga teachers to clearly describe how the practice of yoga and its philosophy can lead one down the path to wellbeing. Yoga isn't just about moving through a series of poses called *āsanas* or the practice of meditation. Yoga is a philosophy developed over millennia that is based on conversations among people from many cultures on how to better know oneself and interact with others. It is clear to me that *āsanas* and meditation without accompanying yoga philosophy results in that vehicle driving toward wellbeing as running on flat tires. Finally, Bill provides very welcome guidance to those like me who are new to yoga and perhaps a little shy about exposing themselves. It pushed me over the self-imposed barrier of reluctance to participate.

A Manual for Wellbeing matters. It can lead one, as it has for me, to finding that elusive "something missing" that adds to life's quality and meaning. Relatively speaking, I'm early in my learning and practice of the tenets Bill espouses in this book. I am eager to see what happens as I move forward on fully inflated tires. I'm already nicer, more thoughtful and like Bill, smile more.

—Thomas Storer, PhD, Director, Exercise Physiology Laboratory,
Men's Health, Aging, and Metabolism,
Brigham and Women's Hospital, Boston, Massachusetts

Part 1

Wellbeing Explained

Chapter 1
What is wellbeing?

If I asked you "Would you like to live a life of wellbeing?" I bet you would readily say, "Yes, of course!" And, why wouldn't you? It sounds great. But what does "wellbeing" really mean? What does a life of wellbeing look like?

To the degree we give wellbeing any thought at all, many of us probably think of it as generally feeling "happy." For some people happiness is living in a comfortable home, having a satisfying career, owning a few cars and other toys in the garage, traveling to exciting destinations, and enjoying financial security. Others of us likely include in our definition things like physical and mental health, a warm family life, good, supporting relationships, and freedom from stress.

These factors pretty much summed up the way I thought of wellbeing for the longest time. When I was in college in the late 1960's, my thoughts were primarily on playing football, studying, and having a good time. My plans for "down the road" involved pursuing a career that would provide a nice, comfortable future, getting married and starting a family, as well as keeping fit and healthy. Providing for that family and that life—not a passion for the law—were the main reasons I decided to go to law school.

I got married, did well in law school, graduating in 1975, joined a law firm, and started a family. I stayed fit and healthy, playing basketball, lifting weights, running, and practicing karate. Over the years, I reached a level of financial security as a trial attorney and partner in a high-profile national law firm. Despite living what I thought was "the dream," I was surprised, after a while, to find myself increasingly haunted each year by a nagging voice telling me I was missing something in my life, an important something. I found myself with greater frequency wondering if there must be something more to life and pondering what that might be.

At the same time, I struggled with the stress of my job. There is quite a bit of stress involved with being a trial lawyer, just like there is, I'm sure, with any number of other jobs. In addition to the challenges of the work itself, I felt anxiety trying to climb the ladder of success in my law firm, even after being named a partner. There was pressure to bring in more clients, keep the existing ones happy, and increase profit. As a busy trial attorney, I was racing through life, from one project to another, constantly worried and distracted by concerns over what deadlines I might be missing, and how I could get a dozen things done at once. After some time, I began to notice that I was neglecting my friends, even my family. Occasionally, when I stopped for a breath, I would ask myself when I had last had a good laugh, gone for a relaxing walk, or paused to simply unwind. Eventually, my marriage ended.

I could see I was heading in the wrong direction. I finally said "enough!" and made a commitment to figure out what the "something more" must be that was so obviously missing from my life. I chose to turn my life around. I wasn't sure how to do that, because I had no roadmap or manual to point the way, but I knew the first step was to find a way to relax. Sometime during 1997 a friend of mine, Jim, a pharmacist and real estate entrepreneur, convinced me to begin taking yoga classes. He told me that yoga helped him relax in the face of all the stress he faced and that it had taught him how to stop and "smell the roses" of life. That sounded like exactly what I needed, so I started going to yoga classes with him, one night a week.

Right away I began to experience what Jim was talking about. There was something about doing yoga poses that resonated with me. I felt at peace watching the movements of my breath, forgetting for a while the demands of my law practice. There was something about trying to coordinate my breath while trying to align various parts of my body that left me relaxed and even, on occasion, serene. I knew I was on to something and so I soon started attending additional classes each week. I even started to drop in at yoga classes in other cities while traveling on business. I found yoga classes were an oasis of freedom from stress and worry. I didn't even mind that my body couldn't do many of the poses the way the other men and women could. I was so hungry for a way to relax that my normally bossy ego took a vacation during each class. Before long I found that even outside of class my mind became less dominated by the stressful, distracting, and constant chattering of my thoughts.

As my stress levels began to diminish, my enjoyment of life began to increase. My partners, associates, staff, and even opposing lawyers encouraged me to stick with yoga. In fact, a few of the lawyers I ran up against on cases started asking me what I had been doing to calm down. A few even asked me what I was "taking," thinking I must have started some medication to relax. The feedback didn't come only at work. With my mind less controlled by stress, I started paying more attention to what people were saying, including my son, friends, and even strangers. I also started noticing life more, including the so-called "little" things that really add spice to life, like the taste of my food, the pleasant aromas of the bakery, the innovative architectural design of a building, little kids having fun, and the uplifting laughter of a group enjoying themselves. Who knew?

I was so taken with yoga that I started attending workshops on yoga philosophy somewhere around 2001 or 2002. I was fascinated and inspired by the focus on helping students discover their potential and manifest that potential in some meaningful way. This philosophy offered me a glimpse of what my own life could be. I started asking myself fundamental questions such as: "who am I" and "what do I want out of my life?" **I began to suspect that the "something more" that appeared so allusive to me was discovering what I was capable of doing in the world and finding a way to express those things regularly in my life.** Being committed to turning my life around, finding the "something more" and getting on the right track, I knew I needed to first figure out who I was and what my full potential was, and then find ways to develop and share it for the rest of my life.[1]

---

1. As I discuss later, there are many yoga traditions, each with varying and sometimes quite dissimilar philosophical viewpoints. The teacher who first opened my eyes to the potential of yoga as a means for living a life rich in wellbeing is Dr. Douglas Brooks, Professor of Religion at the University of Rochester. Dr. Brooks is a scholar of Hinduism, south Asian languages, and the comparative study of religions. For more information about Dr. Brooks and his perspective on yoga philosophy, visit his website at https://rajanaka.com; retrieved November 29, 2018. Studying with Dr. Brooks led me to pursue the study of Anusara yoga, the style of yoga in which I am certified. I spent many hours in philosophy workshops taught by Anusara yoga's founder, John Friend, and a number of his senior teachers, as well as workshops and retreats taught by Dr. Brooks and other scholars such as Dr. Paul Muller-Ortega, Dr. William Mahony, and Sally Kempton, among others.

I enrolled in graduate school at St. Mary's University in Minnesota, even as I continued my full-time law practice and the study and practice of yoga. My graduate work led to a master's degree in Human Development in 2005. During my studies, I focused on human behavior and, specifically, how yoga, including the study of yoga philosophy, can positively impact behavior. My graduate work culminated in my final position paper: "The Role of Yoga in Personal Transformation" which led to the release of my first book in 2013.[2] In that book I used stories, often from my own life as an accomplished but highly stressed-out trial lawyer, to show how yoga practice and philosophy can help us relax and awaken to our own potential and more fully experience life.

After I completed graduate school, I continued to explore behavioral science, particularly the area of positive psychology, a field devoted to the scientific study of the characteristics that allow individuals and communities to thrive.[3] In my ongoing research I came across a 2011 book, *Flourish*,[4] by an author and professor whose work I'd studied in graduate school, Dr. Martin Seligman. Dr. Seligman is a past President of the American Psychological Association (1998), and one of his key contributions to the field of behavior is the promotion of positive psychology as a field of scientific study.[5] I was impressed with his views on what makes life most worth living, including how people can learn to better understand themselves as well as create more positive connection with others. With that in mind, I eagerly read *Flourish*, looking forward to learning about what he referred to as his "wellbeing theory."[6]

2. Dorigan, William (2013). *Finding the Midline*. Winter Park, CO: LuHen Publications, LLC.

3. University of Pennsylvania, Positive Psychology Center; www.ppc.sas.upenn.edu; retrieved June 9, 2018.

4. Seligman, Dr. Martin (2011). *Flourish*. New York, NY: The Free Press.

5. www.ppc.sas.upenn.edu/people/martin-ep-seligman; retrieved June 9, 2018.

6. *Flourish*, at 14-15 (identifying the five elements of Dr. Seligman's wellbeing theory).

Dr. Martin Seligman's wellbeing theory.

Dr. Seligman's wellbeing theory consists of five distinct elements: **1) positive emotions**; including, by way of example, happiness and life satisfaction, along with emotions such as pride, gratitude, joy, and wonder; **2) engagement**; those times when we get so lost in a challenging activity that time flies and our mind becomes totally absorbed in what we are doing; **3) meaning**; using our strengths to create value that serves something greater than just ourselves; **4) accomplishments**; starting and completing a task, small or large, we choose to undertake simply because we feel like it; and **5) positive relationships**; experiencing life in healthy relationship with others, rather than in solitude.[7] Part 1 of this book is directed to describing each of these elements in detail.

These five elements further the goal of the positive psychology movement "to measure and build human flourishing" not only in our own lives, but also "on the planet."[8] The elements are founded on the notion of "uncoerced choice," meaning each of these elements are "what free people will choose for their own sake."[9] Research demonstrates that our human nature isn't simply to choose activities that increase our happiness or make us feel good.[10] Rather, when we are free to make choices about how to direct our time, energy, and resources—how to fully express ourselves—we will, in addition to finding ways to feel good, also undertake challenging and engaging activities, find meaningful ways to contribute to others, pursue successful completion of goals that interest us, and seek connection with people who care about us and support us.[11]

---

7. *Flourish*, at 13–20 (describing each element of the wellbeing theory).

8. *Flourish*, at 26–29.

9. *Flourish*, at 16.

10. *Flourish*, at 24 (distinguishing the wellbeing theory from the "one-dimensional" authentic happiness theory which focuses solely on making choices that cause us to "maximize how we feel," while ignoring our drive to express ourselves in other ways, such as through engagement and accomplishment).

11. *Flourish*, at 16–20; 24–29 (elaborating on the requirement of "uncoerced choice" as an underpinning of each element of the wellbeing theory).

Importantly, a key component of this particular wellbeing theory is that true wellbeing comes from an approximate balance of these elements, not just the pursuit of some of them to the exclusion of others. It is the total contribution from each element that defines wellbeing,[12] with no single element being determinative of whether a person's life is rich in wellbeing. For example, a person might be quite successful in racking up accomplishments in his or her life. However, this success can actually diminish wellbeing if, in order to achieve goals that person sacrifices the regular experience of one or more of the other four elements, such as meaning or positive relationships. When setting our "life course," we as humans flourish when we "maximize all five of these elements."[13]

Calibrating towards greater wellbeing.

Decades of research in behavioral psychology as well as centuries of lessons from yoga philosophy tell us that perhaps our deepest urge as human beings is to recognize and manifest our full potential. It is our human nature to be all we can be. No wonder this was the recruiting slogan of the United States Army for so many years. It touches us down deep at our core. University of Alabama football coach Nick Saban said it another way recently in an interview when asked how he manages to keep his players at such a high level of commitment week after week, season after season (five national championships since 2008 and close to fifty first team All-Americans). He responded by saying that he regularly challenges each player to ask themselves if they are living in each moment as the best version of themselves that they can be. After studying Dr. Seligman's theory of wellbeing, I realized that the inner voice I'd been hearing over the years was this very desire in me, telling me that despite my accomplishments, I was capable of being "something more."

---

12. *Flourish*, at 15.

13. *Flourish*, at 25 (stating that in order to maximize wellbeing we must look beyond what simply makes us feel good to also consider the real-world impact of our life; i.e., do we truly create meaning in what we do, are our relationships healthy, and have we accomplished things?).

These five elements of wellbeing represent those five areas of our lives that, through proper attention and skillful application, allow us to bring out our best as human beings. They collectively identify those areas of our lives, research tells us, we as humans most long to fill—assuming we have awakened to our own inner voice. They are the roadmap for each of us to the "something more" we are capable of being. For example, in Chapter 2 and throughout this book you'll learn about the many ways human beings can experience positive emotions. Positive emotions are far more than laughing regularly and feeling happy. Rather, they are some of the most profound emotions a person can experience, made even more so when experienced with others. They occur when we connect most deeply to ourselves and, when shared with another human being, foster some of the most intimate moments of relationship life offers.

In the discussion of engagement in Chapter 3 you will learn how engagement challenges us to achieve a higher expression of ourselves. By choosing to regularly add engaging activities to our lives we will necessarily undertake ongoing inner examination of our capabilities, followed by challenging ourselves to express those capabilities. In Chapter 4 you'll learn, perhaps surprisingly, that we each have an inner drive to live with purpose, to be a meaningful person. This drive, if we seek to nurture it and allow it to flourish, allows us to not only express ourselves, but to do so in a way that serves something bigger than ourselves. In Chapter 5 you'll see in the discussion of accomplishments that human beings are wired to achieve, which again can result in an ongoing inner dialogue and personal challenge for full expression. As humans, we want to succeed, we want to win. And, in Chapter 6 you'll learn about the value and necessity of positive human connection with others.

Each of these five elements reflects our human desire for full expression in the world. Each requires a process through which we become the best we can be in that moment: allowing ourselves to experience the positive emotions of life, as opposed to remaining numb to them; spending time challenging our talents and preferences through engaging activities; doing something of value to others; achieving a goal; and connecting intimately with others, as opposed to experiencing the ups and downs of life alone. By finding a way to calibrate our choices towards experiencing each of these elements in some approximate balance, we become the best version of ourselves that we can be.[14] This book is written to help you in this process, providing you with the information necessary to make these calibrations yourself.

To demonstrate how this calibration of the five elements can work, I'll give you a few examples from my own life. I identified two elements, positive emotions, and relationships, where I was really out of balance. In addition, while not so obvious at first, I eventually identified two additional elements in need of some calibration, meaning and accomplishments. Let me explain.

First, I saw that I was that person racking up accomplishment after accomplishment to the detriment of my overall wellbeing, specifically in the area of positive relationships. As I said earlier, despite these accomplishments I knew something was missing. As cliché as it sounds, I knew I was not "complete." As a result of my research into the elements of the Seligman wellbeing theory, I realized that I was neglecting my personal relationships, both in terms of developing new friendships and nurturing existing ones. I was reminded of the value of warm relationships in my life. I could see I needed to begin making choices on how to spend my time and energy in a way that developed and sustained supporting, positive relationships. I would have to let go of my innate desire to chase every goal.

To help me make this personal calibration, I began to gauge my daily choices in these terms: Would what I was about to do or say enhance or hinder my personal connection with others. For example, when I am tempted to pursue a new goal, such as certification in another style of yoga, I stop and ask myself if the value of accomplishing this new goal outweighs the value of spending time visiting my grandkids, hanging out with friends, or doing something else that builds connection with people. The answer these days is usually pretty obvious to me, now that I have the habit of calibrating, and I choose to build and nurture my positive relationships instead of chasing after quite as many goals.

---

14. *Flourish*, at 15 (stating that each element contributes to wellbeing, but none define wellbeing).

In my mindfulness inventory of myself, I recognized that I was doing only marginally better in the area of positive emotions, the subject of the next chapter. For example, I seldom, if ever, allowed myself time to feel joy about anything, even when I achieved a major goal. I remember testing for my first black belt in Shotokan karate in front of karate master Hidetaka Nishiyama. When my instructor informed me in front of the whole class, that I had passed and that Sensei Nishiyama had been impressed with my reverse punch, I was emotionally numb. I didn't pause to appreciate the compliment, a real honor from such a highly-regarded master. I felt no joy or pride, nor did I feel any gratitude towards my teachers and fellow students with whom I had trained for so long. Instead, the first feeling I recall was a commitment welling up inside me as I stood there to attend more classes, practice harder, and study more, so I could pass the Second Dan rank test when I became eligible in a couple of years. I was so "wired to succeed" that my brain didn't allow me even a moment to savor this accomplishment. Rather than relish this achievement, I did what I always did after accomplishing a goal, big or small; I immediately turned my attention to the next goal without pausing to appreciate the one just attained.

Here's another example. I recall one particular occasion in which my law firm and I were able to force a builder's insurance company to pay several million dollars to repair construction mistakes at a condominium project. When we visited the homeowners to give them the great news, more than one of them broke into tears, hugging us as they thanked us for saving their largest lifetime investment, their homes. Again, numb, I nodded, and went on my way.

Missing opportunities such as these for connection—not only connection with others but also with my own emotions—was no way to live, no way to flourish. I again used my mindfulness inventory to calibrate my life towards greater wellbeing, in this case by focusing on actually experiencing positive emotions rather than ignoring them. I decided to create a habit of taking a "time out," no matter how brief, after accomplishing any task, to ask myself how I felt about what I just did. I waited until I felt an answer inside me. Sometimes it was pride. Other times it was amusement, or gratitude such as the time my neighbor had to rescue me from a cooking experiment. Over time, this practice has become a habit, and laughing, feeling grateful, becoming awestruck at something, and other positive emotions come easier to me. And the reward for regularly experiencing positive emotions is far more than feeling good in the moment. As I explain later, positive emotion can be contagious. Before I knew it, people started to spend more time around me, no doubt because there was a greater likelihood that we'd share a laugh or maybe an inspiring story.

Sometimes a lack of balance in the five elements is not as easy to identify as was the case with me and the elements of relationships and positive emotions. Let me give you another example from my own life. Over time I began to see how my law practice didn't completely satisfy my needs to fully express myself, to be the best version of me. In many ways my career as a trial lawyer was a good match for me. My job frequently satisfied my curiosity and urge to create. These are significant driving forces in me.[15] The work we did as lawyers in helping others was certainly meaningful. On the other hand, my job often weighed heavily on me for a number of reasons, including the stress and tension generated by our constant need to win. After all, people were paying us and relying on us to help them. This required that we had to be constantly on the lookout for all that could go wrong. We had to anticipate the worst. So, in part to find an outlet that offered doses of optimism and playfulness, other needs important to me, I signed up for a yoga teacher training at CorePower Yoga in Denver. After completing the training, I began teaching yoga, first for that studio, and then, soon thereafter, at other studios around town and up in the mountains in Winter Park, Colorado. I found that I loved teaching yoga for a number of reasons, including the fact that it offered me a way to spend time with people promoting optimism and good cheer, assisting students as they sought to feel better, have a nice time, and gain more flexibility and health. I loved teaching the philosophy and engaging in the give and take of discussions about it. Like my law practice, teaching yoga created meaning in my life. However, unlike my law practice, I was able to count on regular weekly doses of humor, hope, playfulness, and thoughtful interaction about the highest nature of human beings. By finding this outlet I was able to keep the lawyer job I needed and wanted while at the same time bringing myself into a rough balance of all five elements of wellbeing.

---

15. In Chapter 3 I mention an on-line self-evaluation for identifying our personal character strengths and virtues, those traits that most define us, and I provide a link directing you to the site where you can do your own self-evaluation.

As I've illustrated here with a few examples, these five elements of wellbeing offer each of us a way to calibrate our own lives towards greater wellbeing. They offer a pathway to identifying who we are, what we want, and then meaningfully expressing that version of us in the world, enjoying life in the process.

In Part 1 of this book I explain each of the five elements of wellbeing. I provide you with a clear pathway towards building your own life of wellbeing. And, in Part 2 I explain how yoga teaches three skills necessary to successfully navigate that path, calibrating your choices as necessary so you can best utilize the information you learn in Part 1 to build that life. [16]

Why yoga for building wellbeing?

Building a life rich in wellbeing requires more than just an intellectual understanding of the theory. **No matter how much we understand each of the elements of wellbeing, we require three skills in order to fully implement that understanding—awareness of what is going on around us as well as self-awareness, the ability to sustain a focus, and being able to effectively connect with ourselves and with others.** [17]

---

16. There are certainly other worthwhile theories of wellbeing. For example, Dr. Deepak Chopra, author, physician, and health advocate, proposed "The Five Pillars of Radical Wellbeing" consisting of proper sleep, mediation, physical movement, healthy emotions, and eating fresh, real food. You can find his discussion of this theory on-line: http://chopra.com/sites/default/files/TMBD-S1-TheFivePillarsOfRadicalWell-being.pdf; retrieved November 30, 2018. Another theory of wellbeing is offered in the best-selling book: Covey, Stephen R. (2004 ed.). *The 7 Habits of Highly Effective People*. New York, NY: Simon and Schuster, at 299-319 (suggesting a theory of wellbeing as his seventh habit, a process of self-renewal consisting of taking care of our self physically (exercise, nutrition, and stress management), socially/emotionally, spiritually, including meditation, and mentally, including reading and visualization). Yet another set of elements for wellbeing is discussed in Blackburn, Dr. Elizabeth and Epel, Dr. Elissa (2018). *The Telomere Effect*. New York, NY: Grand Central Publishing, at 172–185; 207–242 (reporting on research demonstrating the vital role of exercise, including cardiovascular and strength training, along with good nutrition and stress management, for increased health and immunity).

17. Siegel, Dr. Daniel J. (2018). *Aware*. New York, NY: Penguin Random House, at 4–5 (discussing the Greek term eudaimonia, referring to a sense of wellbeing, equanimity, and happiness that arises when we live a life of meaning and connection to others and the world around us. Dr. Siegel refers to scientific studies supporting the proposition that the

The first skill is awareness. We must be awake enough in each moment to recognize and respond effectively to life's invitations to experience wellbeing. For example, if we aren't awake to our surroundings, we will miss opportunities to experience more positive emotions. Or, chances to provide some meaningful service to our community will escape our attention. Similarly, we'll miss out on engaging activities. Occasions for setting worthwhile goals will elude us. Moments ripe for deepening relationships will pass us by.

In addition, we need to develop self-awareness, understanding our habitual patterns of thinking, the way we view the world. These patterns are the "old tapes" some therapists reference that consist of self-limiting emotions and attitudes we've developed about ourselves or others over our lifetime. Such emotions and attitudes can include anger, lack of self-worth, fear, and prejudices. Only through a refined sense of self-awareness can we recognize in the present moment—and then overcome—these old habits of thinking that can sabotage our efforts at building wellbeing. I address these patterns in detail in Chapter 7. And, as we will see in Part 2, yoga is unparalleled for developing the level of awareness we need to recognize and embrace invitations for wellbeing as well as freeing ourselves of the obstacles our old patterns of thought can throw in our way.

The second skill we need is the ability to sustain a focus on whatever we choose to do. Focus allows us to follow whatever choice we make through to completion. It does us little good to develop a heightened sense of awareness for the opportunities life offers, if, once we choose to pursue an opportunity, we soon drop the ball. It takes the skill of sustained focus to fully cultivate the elements of wellbeing, to keep our mind engaged in the task at hand, whether it is paying attention to somebody telling an inspiring story or an amusing joke, giving an activity enough time to grab our full attention, or following up on getting to know somebody who impressed us as a person. Yoga is tailor-made for increasing an ability to focus.

And the third skill we need to maximize wellbeing is the ability to more effectively connect with our self and with others. This allows us to

---

three skills of open awareness, focused attention, and kindness, lead to greater wellbeing, significant improvements in physical and mental health, as well as various markers for healthy aging).

recognize our full potential and meaningfully express it in the world, living as an inspiration to others. As we will see throughout this book, particularly in Chapter 10, yoga philosophy offers centuries of valuable insight into identifying our highest nature as human beings, fully connecting to ourselves in a way we've likely not yet experienced. It also offers us lessons on creating greater harmony in our interaction with others, significantly increasing the opportunity for wellbeing in our lives.

Further, we'll see in Part 2 how yoga practices and the lessons of yoga philosophy are of great assistance in helping us more effectively connect with others. We learn from yoga how to refine our behavior in such a way that we attract others and, through that attraction, increase our opportunities for experiencing positive emotions, engagement, accomplishment, meaning, and positive relationships.

Part 1 gives you a roadmap for enriching your life with wellbeing. And, Part 2 teaches how yoga practices and yoga philosophy help you calibrate your thoughts and behavior in a way that maximizes wellbeing in your life. For these reasons, consider this book a manual for wellbeing; it is a "how to" book for enhancing the presence of each element of wellbeing in your life.

Let's begin our study of wellbeing by exploring the first element, positive emotions.

Chapter 2
Positive emotions

Happiness is an emotion many of us immediately think of when we first hear the term "wellbeing." Being happy is certainly a positive emotion. But positive emotions also include feelings such as "pleasure, rapture, ecstasy, warmth, comfort, and the like."[18] They help create "the pleasant life."[19]

However, there are other emotions that also help enrich our lives and it is these I discuss in this chapter. Those positive emotions are: joy, gratitude, serenity, interest, hope, pride, amusement, inspiration, awe, and love.[20] This list is based on research finding these to be the ten positive emotions that "color people's day-to-day lives the most."[21] I describe each in some detail below.

Before looking at each of these ten positive emotions, note that **the value of positive emotions goes beyond simple appreciation for whatever nice mood we're experiencing in the moment. Positive emotions have the power to transform our lives.** Many of us fall victim to our own patterns of negative thoughts and emotions, such as feelings of unworthiness, fear,

---

18. *Flourish*, at 11.

19. *Flourish*, at 16 (describing the "pleasant life" to include happiness and life satisfaction).

20. This list is derived from work discussed by Dr. Barbara Fredrickson in her book *Positivity*: Fredrickson, Dr. Barbara (2009). *Positivity*. New York, NY: Three Rivers Press, at 39–48. Dr. Fredrickson, a leading expert on the subject of positive psychology and emotional positivity, is the Principal Investigator at the University of North Carolina's Positive Emotions and Psychophysiology Lab. The Lab studies how positive emotions affect people and how such emotions can work "to transform people's lives for the better." The following link directs you to the University of North Carolina, Positive Emotions and Psychophysiology Laboratory ("PEP" Lab): http://peplab.web.unc.edu/1; retrieved June 10, 2018.

21. *Positivity*, at 39 (referring to research involving the daily emotional experiences of hundreds of people across a broad age spectrum).

anger, bias, envy, greed, or any number of other often unhelpful ways of thinking and feeling. For example, a feeling of unworthiness can interfere with our ability to pursue the career of our dreams. When we hear of a job opening for a position that appeals to us, we don't even bother to apply because some negative internal voice, part of a pattern from our past, tells us we're not good enough.[22]

In addition to holding us back from pursuing wellbeing, negative patterns of thought and emotion, such as anger, can sometimes cause us to say or do something that creates all sorts of trouble. Have you ever lashed out at someone in anger, only to immediately regret it? But, too late, the words are out there causing hurt and quite possibly destroying the relationship. The more firmly and pervasively these negative patterns have taken root, the more unlikely it will be that we make much progress in developing solid positive relationships until we identify and overcome them.

It isn't easy to eliminate these negative patterns. In fact, scientists tell us that feelings of negativity are actually more intense than positive feelings. This is called a "negativity bias."[23] When the mind wanders, it tends to gravitate towards unpleasant thoughts or feelings, ruminating over them, and potentially leading, if unattended, to a general state of unhappiness.[24]

If we aren't aware of these patterns and learn to deal with them, negative thoughts and emotions can eventually far outnumber any positive emotions we might have. As a result, we end up plodding along through

---

22. Emotions we might normally classify as negative can be valuable to us in a number of ways, so we always want to pay attention to them whenever they arise in order to figure out what they are telling us. For example, anger can be a very powerful aid in certain situations, helping us stand up for ourselves or others when circumstances require. I wrote about this subject in Chapter 39 of *Finding the Midline*, pointing out that anger "is important, in part because it provides a signal to us that something inside us has been deeply stirred." *Finding the Midline*, at 135. Because of that fact, anger can be our very powerful ally or a very dangerous adversary. Similarly, so-called negative emotions, such as fear and disgust, among others, can be tools "for realigning our life into a different direction." *Finding the Midline*, at 135.

23. *Positivity*, at 130; 144.

24. Goleman, Dr. Daniel (2013). *Focus*. New York, NY: HarperCollins, at 47–48 (reporting that "people's moods were generally skewed to the unpleasant" when the mind is allowed to wander).

life overwhelmed with such depressing negativity that we become pessimists about everything. This type of pattern could even drive us into depression. The prospect of living a life rich in wellbeing then drifts well off our radar screen.

To combat the tendency to dwell in negativity, we can learn to employ a "Positivity Ratio."[25] To do this we teach ourselves to recognize each time a negative thought or feeling arises. In response to the negative thought or feeling, we then try to experience at least three "heartfelt positive emotional experiences" for every single "negative emotional experience" we have.[26] This ratio is designed to help us lessen the effects of the naturally occurring negative emotions in our lives by creating a significantly greater number of positive emotions.[27] To help us in this process we can even create what I call a "wellspring" of positive emotions, a resource of positivity we can draw from, as we need.

For example, consider the positive emotion of gratitude.[28] I don't think it is even possible to be both grateful for something and angry or upset in the same exact moment. For this reason, dealing with moments of anger, it is of great help to have a readily available wellspring of memories of things for which you are grateful. You can even write down such memories of gratitude and keep a list on your desk and carry it in your wallet or purse. Then, consider any feeling of anger to be an automatic signal to reach for the list. In time, the list will reside within you, making it unnecessary to even have a physical reminder. I've done this myself. To create my list, I only had to think of certain of my teachers, my family, and the good fortune I've had in athletics and in other areas of my life. When I feel myself becoming angry, by remembering someone or something I'm grateful for, my mind has no space left over for whatever negative outburst is trying to envelope me. I transform the negative thinking into a positive emotion of gratitude.

---

25. *Positivity*, at 16.

26. *Positivity*, at 32 (describing a 3 to 1 ratio for matching each negative emotional experience with at least three "heartfelt positive emotional experiences that uplift" us).

27. *Positivity*, at 120–138 (providing examples of application of the positivity ratio).

28. *Positivity*, at 179–198. Dr. Fredrickson's book is a vital resource for learning how to employ positive emotions to increase our wellbeing. She explains how to create a "toolkit" in Chapter 11 for use in changing our negativity/positivity ratio. *Positivity*, at 199–223.

When we learn to successfully employ the use of the Positivity Ratio in our life, including the use of our own wellspring of positive emotions, our mind becomes uncluttered by negativity and is free to use positive emotions as a springboard to "unleashing the flourishing possibilities" in our lives.[29] For example, by cultivating the positive emotion of interest we become curious, opening our minds to more of what life has to offer. When we go to a party, we can choose to be interested in those at the party we don't know and who don't seem, for whatever reason, to be like people we would normally spend time with. Why is he here? What does the host see in her? Inevitably, because the world is full of interesting people with experiences we often can't begin to imagine, we'll meet some intriguing people. We may even make a new friend. Or, at a minimum, we might learn about some travel destination, occupation, hobby, or something else we know nothing about. Who knows? We quite likely will learn something.[30] As an additional benefit of being a curious person, we ourselves become more interesting to others as we assimilate more and more information about a wide range of topics, all gleaned from extending ourselves in order to meet people outside our normal sphere of interest. This, in turn, opens the door to even more positive relationships, more wellbeing, as people become drawn to us.

Another way of unleashing our flourishing possibilities is to engage in those "random acts of kindness" you see mentioned on bumper stickers. Research suggests that the more we engage in kindness the more our levels of "positivity" increase.[31] Take time to observe people as you walk down the street, hallway, or aisles, and notice when somebody looks a bit sad. In a simple, nonintrusive way, offer them a smile or pleasant nod as you continue on your way. There's a fair chance you'll favorably shift their mood. And, borrowing a timeless lesson from yoga's *Bhagavad Gita*, don't

---

29. *Positivity*, at 179 (reporting research indicating that applying the positivity ratio not only makes us happier, but also makes us more creative and resilient, and increases our capacity to provide meaningful service).

30. *Positivity*, at 194–196 (explaining some values of having an open mind).

31. *Positivity*, at 197, *citing* Otake, K., S. Shimai, et al. (2006). "Happy people become happier through kindness: A counting kindness intervention." *Journal of Happiness Studies* 7:361–75.

be concerned about whether the person responds favorably or not.[32] The mission here is for you to deepen your experience of being kind.

We can enrich our lives in many other ways through use of the Positivity Ratio. For example, when we experience a setback, we learn to look for a "silver lining" in the situation. We do this to be hopeful, reminding ourselves that whatever is going on will have an end to it.[33] As we will see later, cultivating an attitude of hope in the face of potential despair is believed to be critical to good health. Another reason for looking for a silver lining is to identify something positive we can gain from the experience. When I broke my leg, I realized that I now had plenty of time to increase my upper body mobility through my yoga practice. The broken leg became a blessing in the sense that finally I could concentrate on making my spine more limber. It became an even greater blessing when I found out how generous my neighbors were. Because of the broken leg I made new friends with whom I spend a great deal of time today. I used the setback of a broken leg to calibrate myself into greater wellbeing by both improving my yoga practice and increasing positive relationships in my life.

Let's look in detail at each of these ten most common positive emotions.

Joy.

Joy is a feeling of elation. It occurs when we feel safe and things are going our way. We often experience joy when we receive an unexpected and pleasant surprise that delights us. We feel playful, vibrant, and aglow.[34]

---

32. Abhinavagupta (2004 ed). *Gitartha Samgraha. Abhinavagupta's Commentary on the Bhagavad Gita* (B. Marjanovic, Trans.). New Delhi, India: First Impression, at 67 (translation and commentary on Chapter 2, Verse 48: "Your domain is the field of action alone, and never its fruits. Do not be motivated by the fruits of action, nor attached to inaction").

33. *Positivity*, at 182 (explaining that while looking for the positive may not, in and of itself, resolve the immediate problem, doing so can unleash "positive dynamics" that reverse the course of negativity).

34. *Positivity*, at 40–41.

When I read this definition, I immediately thought of a moment from a professional football game I watched in late December 2017. The Buffalo Bills' twelve-year veteran 303-pound defensive tackle Kyle Williams lined up in the backfield at the goal line against the Miami Dolphins in a late season game that would determine if the Bills made the playoffs for the first time since 1999. Rumor had it that Williams intended to retire at the end of the season, so this was potentially the last game he would ever play. As a defensive lineman, he had never scored a touchdown in his entire pro career. But here he was lined up in the backfield as a running back with the game on the line.

Williams took the handoff and bulldozed right through the Dolphins' defenders for a one-yard touchdown. Even sitting in my easy chair, I could feel the collective joy of Williams and his teammates as they did a goofy and carefree celebration in the end zone. They were expressing a spontaneous explosion of joy. The Bills went on to win that game, making the playoffs. Joy can be contagious, as I found myself laughing along with the Bills' players and Williams in their playful touchdown dance.

Joy is not only a "fun" or playful feeling. It is also a powerful feeling in ways we may not realize. We can experience the power of joy whenever we creatively express ourselves in some meaningful way. **Arguably, our deepest desire is to uncover our true potential and manifest it, whether through work or an avocation. In fact, it is a "central need" of human beings to bring our potential into action.**[35] This expression of our potential has been called the "most alive feeling of power" and stems from satisfying this primal desire to be everything we are capable of being. This feeling of self-affirming power is considered the "essence of joy"[36] arising from the gratifying recognition that we are, indeed, a person "of worth and dignity."[37] That is what I mean when I say that the positive emotion of joy is powerful.

---

35. May, Dr. Rollo (1983). *The Discovery of Being.* New York, NY: W.W. Norton & Company, Inc., at 80 (citing Nietzsche for the proposition that a human's "fundamental drive" is to "live out one's *potentia*," emphasis in original).

36. *The Discovery of Being*, at 80–83.

37. May, Dr. Rollo (1953). *Man's Search for Himself.* New York, NY: Dell Publishing, at 96 (writing that when we "fill our potentialities as persons, we experience the profoundest joy to which the human being is heir...which accompanies our fulfilling our natures as human beings").

This process of discovering our potential and expressing it in service to others is sometimes called the "good life."[38] Further, research indicates that finding a way of expressing our potential in an act of kindness towards others "produces the single most reliable momentary increase in well-being of any exercise" tested.[39] Being kind to another creates joy within us.

Simple acts of kindness, sharing our caring nature to offer an emotional lift to another, are a great way to generate a self-affirming and powerful experience of joy. By treating others with kindness, we bring our full potential as a human being into action by offering others a sense of belonging and self-worth. This is an incredibly transformative act on our part, both for us and for others, and another reason why the term "power" is used to describe such moments. Not only do we affirm our own worth and dignity through each act of kindness, we also, at the same time, give others a taste of their worth and dignity. Through each act of kindness, we mold ourselves more and more into the type of person others want to spend time with, want to connect with. And, as we will see in Chapter 6, establishing positive relationships is vital to wellbeing.

Such is the extraordinarily powerful range of joy. It can arise from a random moment, such as watching a football play on television or sharing the elation of a laughing child tottering down the aisle of an airplane. And joy can also be an extremely powerful tool for creating our own life of well-being when we choose to offer our unique set of strengths in furtherance of something bigger than ourselves.[40] Expressing ourselves so fully and powerfully in that way opens the door to an experience of vibrant elation. We can choose to use this power any time we wish.

---

38. *Flourish*, at 17–21; Seligman, Dr. Martin (2002). *Authentic Happiness*. New York, NY: Free Press, at 260 ("The good life consists in deriving happiness by using your signature strengths every day in the main realms of living").

39. *Flourish*, at 20.

40. *Finding the Midline*, at 73–75 (referring to yoga's concept of *Satchitānanda*—truth, consciousness, and bliss—ability to courageously explore our full potential, acknowledge that potential, and then offer that potential in service of something bigger than ourselves).

Gratitude.

Gratitude is a feeling of appreciation for the gifts we receive in life. It is a heartfelt, spontaneous, and pleasant feeling, prompting us to want to reciprocate.[41] This feeling of appreciation is "self-transcendent," meaning that it causes us to look at our relationship and connection to others, rather than just thinking about ourselves.[42] Life's gifts come in all forms, ranging from a new sweater on our birthday to being on the receiving end of one of those random acts of kindness I mentioned earlier.

When we start paying attention, we'll see that these gifts abound. As a trial lawyer I eventually began to notice that the opposing lawyers I had been so tough on were interesting men and women. One night I had to attend a hearing on a case and arrived early. I ran into one of those lawyers I'm talking about, Barry. Barry was a long-time adversary who had been on the receiving end of some of my snarky comments in the past. We started talking and before long the subject got around to karate, which I regularly practiced. Barry told me he had been practicing *Tai Chi* for about 25 years and explained why he liked it so much. He enjoyed how much it simultaneously made him feel strong and powerful while at the same time feeling at peace even when under stress. He was too kind to mention that I may have been one of the causes of that stress.

Before too long I asked him if he could show me "push hands," what I understood to be a very soft, controlled form of "sparring," or fighting. It was something we could do in our suits and ties while we waited for the hearing. We touched forearms and he started to guide me through push hands, smiling and chatting the whole time. I couldn't help myself: I soon tried to nudge him off balance as our arms moved around. Every time I tried to be aggressive, he would make some unseen adjustment and I would start to fall down. He'd easily catch me to keep me upright, all the while easily carrying on our conversation. Undaunted, I would try again, and the same thing would happen. It was like trying to fight with somebody underwater.

---

41. *Positivity*, at 41–42.

42. *Positivity*, at 46–47 (stating that the positive emotions of gratitude, inspiration, and awe are "self-transcendent" because they pull us "out of our shell of self-absorption," connecting us to something larger than ourselves).

We finished, and Barry then described for me what was happening. He was simply reading and accommodating my energy. If I was aggressive, he felt the energy and responded by letting me be the one who lost balance and control. The "life gift" of this interaction for which I am so grateful is when, after we finished our push hands, he told me that in over 25 years of practicing *Tai Chi* he had learned to live life this way. He said this attitude allowed him to surround himself with many kindhearted friends, a loving wife and family, and trustworthy law partners. He was living a life of wellbeing, doing so with a mindset I had never considered—that of being open and accommodating while still being strong and powerful. At any time during our push hands Barry could have wiped me out if it were a real fight; I wouldn't have been able to land a single one of my own well-regarded karate punches. He gave me the gift of seeing a different, healthier way of handling the day to day stresses of being a trial lawyer. And, of course, he gave me a bonus gift of becoming a friend. I remain grateful today for these gifts.

As this story illustrates, it is important that we learn to be aware of what is happening around us, so we can recognize life's gifts whenever they show up. They can appear disguised as people we don't pay much attention to, like Barry, because they are quiet and unassuming. They can show up as beautiful landscaping on the very street we live that we never see because of the phone in our hand. They can emerge in the form of curious questions our kids ask us that we tend to blow off because we're watching a television show. And, of course, they are present as the rainbows, sunrises, sunsets, and all the other wonders of nature that we too often take for granted. They "abound" and they each offer us opportunities to feel grateful for the experience. Each is another gift to our wellspring of gratitude, the one we can draw upon to help transform our disposition into something helpful on our path to greater wellbeing. **As with joy, gratitude is also a powerful emotion because it allows us to transform our attitude in any given moment, reducing or eliminating stress, changing our mood from dark to light, helping us to make choices that support and grow wellbeing.** Let's look further at some examples of the power of gratitude.

I recall one of my teachers telling us about a conversation he had with Swami Chidvilasananda, the spiritual head of the Siddha Yoga tradition. She is better known as Gurumayi Chidvilasananda, or "Gurumayi" (the

Guru immersed in the tradition). My teacher was one of a group of scholars who taught yoga philosophy during summers at the Siddha Yoga ashram, Shree Muktananda Ashram, in upstate New York. Each summer the ashram would fill with visitors coming for retreat. Gurumayi had assembled a team of scholars who lectured on their respective subjects of expertise in yoga philosophy as part of the retreat experience. I'm fortunate, and grateful, in that a number of those scholars later became my teachers.

My teacher described for us how one morning he was sitting privately with Gurumayi in the cafeteria. He was angry about something and was "venting" to her. After quietly listening for a very short while, Gurumayi gently and lovingly stopped him and said something to this effect: "Right now, right here, think of something for which you are grateful. Remember it. Visualize it. Feel the gratitude that arises from it." After a moment or two, she continued: "Notice how gratitude is an elixir; it is, as you sit here, washing the poison right out of your thoughts and off of your tongue. Your whole face is calm again; your body relaxed, and you're even smiling."

That is what I mean by gratitude being a powerful emotion. It is capable of changing the cold steel of our anger or envy, for example, into the shining, beautiful, and valuable gold of a friendly, open, joyful attitude. This is the type of attitude that serves as a critical part of the foundation for a life of wellbeing. It draws people to us, and it opens us to being drawn to others.

How do we better avail ourselves of this powerful elixir of gratitude? We start by developing our ability to be fully aware in each moment so that we don't miss life's gifts; those times in life when we are given something of value, whether it is a smile, a kind word, a compliment, love, attention, praise, advice, or any number of other blessings that come our way. Similarly, we pay attention to those times when luck smiles on us and we avoid problems or even catastrophe. Those times are blessings as well.

For each of these times we teach ourselves to savor these gifts, to fully appreciate what we've been presented. Savoring commits these moments of blessing to memory. By acknowledging and savoring life's gifts to us, we can then develop the wellspring of memories of gratitude I mentioned earlier. Then, we draw upon this wellspring in times of stress, sadness, or other challenges that might otherwise bring us down. When we do so, gratitude arises from this wellspring, "kindled naturally by the recollection of the experiences one has received," releasing the "knots of the heart" to transform negative thinking into a warm, appreciative, useful feeling, the type of feeling that builds and sustains wellbeing.[43]

Serenity.

Serenity is a feeling of calm or peace. We feel trouble-free, relishing the moment. We want to remain in this relaxed, carefree experience and find ways to repeat it more often in the future.[44]

Serenity is a low-key feeling that arises when we feel safe and at ease. Examples include sitting out on the deck enjoying the evening with friends, walking casually through a park on a summer day, or relaxing on our back at the end of a yoga class in a pose called *Śavāsana*.[45] *Śavāsana* is called the "corpse" pose in part because the object is to imitate a corpse as we lie down at the end of class, breathe deeply, and rest. We quiet the mind but are conscious as the body remains still. This pose is refreshing and teaches us to relax.[46] In the pose we learn how to "let go" of the tensions of the day and feel at peace as we relish the moment. Then, refreshed, we arise with a brand-new opportunity to make a life of our choosing.

Although we discuss the value of doing yoga poses later, in Chapter 9, I want to share this brief story of how *Śavāsana* helped teach me to relax. Before finding my way to a yoga class I tried various types of meditation but without much success. Even if I could sit still, I couldn't get my mind

43. Chidvilasananda, Swami (1996). *The Yoga of Discipline*. South Fallsburg, NY: SYDA Foundation, at 135 (referring to the value of drawing upon memory as described in the *Chāndogya Upaniṣad*).

44. *Positivity*, at 42.

45. *Positivity*, at 42.

46. Iyengar, B.K.S. (1979 ed). *Light on Yoga*. New York, NY: Schocken Books, at 422 (describing a benefit of the yoga pose *Śavāsana*: "This conscious relaxation invigorates and refreshes both body and mind").

to calm down. I ruminated over everything, ranging from deadlines for my court cases, what to wear to dinner that night, or when I'd have time to cut the lawn. Various patterns of thoughts like this would run through my mind in no set order, depending on whatever worries or concerns wanted to join in the action.

Eventually I took a Bikram yoga class and this entire mind chattering habit finally met its match. These classes are conducted in a room often heated to slightly over 100 degrees Fahrenheit. The teacher guides the student through a set of 26 poses, two sets each, with little rest between sets, about ten seconds if I recall.

I found that the combination of the hard work of the poses, combined with the heat and little rest, was grueling. I remember that in my first class I was doing okay, getting tired but surviving, until we got to the Dancer pose. In that pose the student stands on one straight leg and reaches the arm on that side of the body out in front. He or she then reaches back and grabs the opposite foot with the other hand and then lifts that back foot up, trying to lift the rear foot towards the ceiling in a backbend. All this is done while attempting to keep the hips and chest pointed forward.

After one set of Dancer Pose, I thought I was going to faint. I stood at attention for the ten-second rest, gasping for air and trying to slow my heart rate down. As I was relishing this tiny 10 second break, this slice of peace and recuperation, my brain began chattering with all sorts of thoughts: "where's the nearest hospital?" "Will I get there in time?" "Can anybody see how out of shape I am?" "What the hell am I doing here?" Desperate for even the briefest moment of peace and quiet, I told my brain to "shut up" because I wanted that precious ten seconds just to rest. I would have used stronger language to my brain, but I was too tired.

Somehow, I made it through the class, getting progressively hotter, sweatier, and more exhausted through each pose. At the end, we laid down for *Śavāsana* and an amazing thing happened. My mind went completely still. I had no energy to even think. At last I had found a way to experience a true moment of peace.

However, the experience wasn't finished. When the teacher told us to roll over and sit up, I couldn't remember ever having felt so relaxed, so at peace, so... serene! I kept going back to Bikram yoga classes in part simply to renew that feeling. Later, as I continued in other styles of yoga and continued to practice meditation, I was able to find feelings of serenity with greater frequency outside of yoga class. The more I practice yoga, including meditation, the easier it has become to experience times of serenity.

Interest.

"Interest" involves situations in which our attention is drawn to something fresh or different. We become fascinated, and are filled with a "sense of possibility," due to whatever has captured our interest.[47]

Interest, or being curious, is of tremendous value in building wellbeing. In yoga philosophy *rasa* is a Sanskrit word meaning "taste, "essence," or, in some cases, the basic feeling or mood of a situation.[48] *Rasas* are the emotional flavors of life, the way we "taste" each experience.[49] I call the *rasas* the "candy store of life" because life offers so many things that can pique our interest if we take time to notice. Paying attention to what draws our attention can give us a glimpse of ourselves, some interest, strength, or passion we might not suspect.

47. *Positivity*, at 43.

48. Feuerstein, Dr. Georg (2001 ed). *The Yoga Tradition*. Prescott, AZ: Hohm Press, at 289 (defining rasa).

49. Chidvilasananda, Swami (1997). *Enthusiam*. South Fallsburg, NY: SYDA Foundation, at 2 (describing *rasa* as a "greater flavor of life"). Often the *rasas* are described as having nine different flavors—peace, compassion, disgust, love, courage, anger, joy, wonder, and fear; *Finding the Midline*, at 134. In Chapter 39 of *Finding the Midline* I discuss each of these emotions. While we see some overlap with Dr. Fredrickson's list of positive emotions; i.e., peace, love, joy, and wonder, the *rasas* encompass a full range of emotional experience, including the so-called "negative" emotions such as disgust, anger, and fear. In *Finding the Midline* I explain how even these negative emotions have value to us and so, in the case of the *rasas*, terminology such as "positive" and "negative" aren't so clearly applicable without determining the full significance of that particular emotional experience; *Finding the Midline*, at 133–136.

Situations exist everywhere for arousing our interest. That's why the *rasas* remind me of a candy store; life offers so many different tempting things to choose from. As we stroll through a bookstore we are attracted to a book and, after reading it, we become hungry to develop a new skill inspired by that book.[50] I recall walking through a bookstore and seeing a book on how to make great stews, chili, and soups in a crock-pot. I was fascinated, and a vision popped into my head of using my nice kitchen to create my own nutritious and delicious meals. So, I bought the book and, soon after, a crock-pot. Now I don't have to wait until the one day each week my local co-op serves chili; I can make it myself. [51]

As we watch kids at a playground, doing cartwheels and backbends, we might become intrigued with the idea of how to develop our own ability to move our body with such freedom. I remember watching Bruce Lee, the martial arts expert, on television playing the character Kato in the *Green Hornet* series. I was so intrigued with his skills that I researched all the different martial arts and eventually went on to study karate and earn three different black belts. Bruce piqued my interest. I wanted to "taste" what it would be like to possess the skills of a martial artist.

As these examples suggest, we increase our wellbeing when we take the time to observe what fascinates us and then explore it as fully as we can. We live in the candy store of life, so the opportunities abound to be fascinated and experience this particular positive emotion of interest. We need to remind ourselves to try new flavors and not always buy the strawberry truffle. Try crème de mint sometime.

---

50. *Positivity*, at 43 (providing examples of the positive emotion of interest, including discovering a new book, spotting a new path in the woods, or accepting a challenge to build a new skill).

51. I first learned about the *rasas* from Dr. Douglas R. Brooks, while on a weekend retreat he held to help explain to us the nuances of discernment—how, by being open to tasting the full array of the flavors life offers, we increase the potential for enriching our lives. To help in that regard, he invited a master sommelier who brought a variety of great wines and conducted wine tastings on Friday and Saturday nights. Dr. Brooks also included a chef who made us wonderful dinners, coordinated with our wines. The retreat offered us the experience of learning how to better identify the wonder and delight in diversity, whether that diversity appears as a red or a white wine, a fine cut of beef and fish, or in people and cultures different from us.

This last point is particularly significant when it comes to being interested in people. People are one of the most intriguing of all subjects to which we can direct our interest. Rather than fear people different from us, the "other," we can challenge ourselves to be especially interested in them and their ideas, to become intensely curious as to why that person believes the way he or she does about something. **By adopting an interest in cultures and ideas different from our own, we eventually will learn to celebrate diversity rather than run from it. We celebrate diversity because we know that hidden within what is unknown to us are the hints of who we might choose to become.**[52] This is how we grow as a person. Through interaction with others spurred on by our interest in what we don't know, we assimilate new ideas and new perspectives. This broadens who we are and what we have to offer the world.

To assist us in broadening ourselves through an increased interest in others, whether strangers or people we know, we can practice what is called "empathetic listening." Unlike other forms of listening, in which we only partially pay attention to what the person is saying, with empathetic listening we listen with not only our ears, but also our eyes and our heart.[53] What do I mean by this?

I mentioned earlier that we as human beings have a strong desire to discover and express our full potential. As a corollary, we also need to be "understood, to be affirmed, and to be validated, to be appreciated."[54] When we engage in empathetic listening, we listen so as to understand the other person from their point of view, how they view the world. This means we set aside our own agenda, including our own perception of what is going on in the moment. We tune in completely to the other person, attempting to not only hear their words and read their facial and

---

52. Brooks, Dr. Douglas R. Public Lecture. Howard, Colorado. July 14, 2011. *See also* Chapter 19 "The Spanda of Relationships," in *Finding the Midline*, at 79–81 (discussing the immense potential for expanding the richness of our life when we open our mind to meeting people different from us).

53. *The 7 Habits of Highly Effective People*, at 252 (describing the skill of empathetic listening).

54. *The 7 Habits of Highly Effective People*, at 253.

bodily expressions, but also to feel what they are feeling. We are attempting to connect to "another human soul."[55]

When we listen to another person this way, we learn to see the world from a new, broader perspective, the perspective of the person with whom we are connecting through our listening. Following our interaction with that person, we no longer see the world only through the lens of our particular experiences because we've assimilated what we've learned from him or her. We've grown as a person by taking the time to explore somebody new and different.

Unless we become fully interested in the world, in what we don't already know, we will never fully develop what we are capable of being. Instead, we will remain mired in what we already are. As great as that might be, it will never be as great as it could be. Somewhere deep within us, we will know that and, in quiet moments, many of us will be troubled by that.

Hope.

We experience "hope" when we are troubled by a situation and not sure things are going to work out the way we want. An example would be when we find out we have been diagnosed with a serious medical condition.[56]

The positive emotions we've looked at so far occur when we are feeling safe and satisfied. Hope is different in that we need hope when we don't feel safe and there is uncertainty looming in our future, even the potential for despair.[57] Without hope, our alternative is hopelessness and depression. Feeling hopeful rather than helpless is part of a resiliency we need to create a life of wellbeing. In challenging times optimists tend more often to thrive whereas pessimists tend to become depressed.[58] In order to increase our

---

55. *The 7 Habits of Highly Effective People*, at 253.

56. *Positivity*, at 43.

57. *Positivity*, at 43. *See also Authentic Happiness*, at 62 (discussing optimism, faith, and trust).

58. Reivich, Dr. Karen and Dr. Andrew Shatte (2002). *The Resilience Factor*. New York,

wellbeing, we have to develop patterns of looking at life in ways that are hopeful rather than helpless, optimistic as opposed to pessimistic. I discuss this in greater detail in Chapter 7 on resiliency.

People who view the world with hope or optimism see the cause of their problems as temporary instead of permanent. For example, a hopeful person who is told he or she has a serious illness will be encouraged and find hope upon learning of others who have overcome the same problem. Conversely, people tending to a sense of helplessness in the face of adversity will more often believe their illness is permanent, even when aware that others have overcome that same illness.[59] **The ability to be hopeful or optimistic is critical not only to wellbeing, but also to our very survival.** Research suggests that there is a positive correlation between optimism and healing,[60] and some well-known health care providers, such as the Mayo Clinic and the Cleveland Clinic, by way of example, place a heavy focus on the role of hope in healing.[61]

Developing the ability to view the world with optimism, with hope, is a key to handling the pitfalls that inevitably appear on our path to wellbeing.

Pride.

NY: Three Rivers Press, at 158 (discussing "explanatory style," the pessimistic or optimistic manner in which a person characterizes a problem they face); *see also Authentic Happiness* at 83 ("Optimism and hope cause better resistance to depression when bad events strike, better performance at work, particularly in challenging jobs, and better physical health").

59. *Authentic Happiness*, at 92.

60. Seligman, Dr. Martin (2006 ed.) *Learned Optimism.* New York, NY: Vintage Books, at 167–184 (reporting the positive health benefits of being optimistic).

61. *See, e.g.,* Mayo Clinic YouTube video and Cleveland Clinic website link pertaining to programs for instilling hope: https://www.youtube.com/user/mayoclinic; retrieved June 19, 2018; https://my.clevelandclinic.org/departments/wellness/integrative/treatments-services/guided-imagery; retrieved June 19, 2018. *See also* Siegel, Dr. Daniel (2011 ed). *Mindsight.* New York, NY: Bantam Books, at 55–56 (discussing research indicating the negative impact of the stress hormone cortisol on our immune systems's ability to fight cancer and other disease).

We can feel pride when we acknowledge we are responsible for achieving something.[62] Examples include completing a degree program, building a new deck at home, and a job well done at work.[63] Pride is defined as a justifiable self-respect. It is a sense of self-esteem, a reasonable feeling of accomplishment. [64]

Pride often gets a bad rap. In fact, it is considered in some religions to be the root of all evil or, at a minimum, one of the "seven deadly sins."[65] For example, I remember as a small boy every time I accomplished something of any merit, I was told not to be "prideful," not to boast, not to be "too big for my britches." I was ordered to instead be quiet and humble. Fortunately, over time I learned that while boasting was obnoxious, an honest and reasonable acknowledgement to myself of a successful effort was important to my sense of self. I also learned that there were plenty of people out there willing to brag about themselves, whether justified or not, and so if I wanted to get ahead, I'd better be sure to let others know that I was capable as well. After doing so much work to discover and share my own potential, my particular strengths, I found that false modesty was a very self-limiting impediment.

To develop a sense of pride, I learned to acknowledge my competency to myself and feel pride in my skill level. I recognized that I had something to offer others, ways to be meaningful. I knew that unless I acknowledged my value to myself, it would be very difficult to convey to others I had something to offer them. Because I want to live a life of purpose, I took a fresh, honest look at my strengths and accepted them as part of who I am.

---

62. *Positivity*, at 44.

63. *Positivity*, at 44 (providing examples of the positive emotion of pride).

64. *Positivity*, at 44–45.

65. *Positivity*, at 44 (discussing how pride has a "mixed reputation, considered in some religious circles to be one of the seven deadly sins); these seven deadly sins are often identified as lust, gluttony, greed, sloth, wrath, envy, and pride, with pride sometimes being considered the worst because it is thought to separate the soul from God.

Pride is a subject that comes up frequently in yoga classes. Fairly often we hear yoga teachers tell their students to make sure ego doesn't get in the way of their pose, or their life, for that matter. Some will even say that ego is a bad thing. I suggest that our pride or ego: "is a gift because it gives us our distinctiveness and personality."[66]

Pride helps give us our drive to succeed, to fully express who we are, to be the best we can be. Pride is "expansive," in that it urges us to further develop our potential.[67] Even after we acknowledge our strengths and capabilities, we will only fully manifest our full potential for greatness if we challenge ourselves and are unwilling to be satisfied with less than our best. How many medical and pharmaceutical discoveries come from people who take pride in the excellence of their intellect and their hunger to live up to their full potential through their research? Their pride helps them overcome failure after failure before succeeding. Absent a healthy sense of pride, I suspect a number of these researchers would give up after the first, second, or third failure, never knowing that the cure for some disease is waiting for their very next laboratory tweak.

Pride or ego only become a problem when "we think the world is only about us" and we lose the "bigger picture of connection," our knowledge that we are part of something bigger than just us.[68] It is in service to that something bigger where we find meaning and it is through effort and risk that we maximize our ability to create meaning. Absent a sense of pride, we are unlikely to put forth that level of effort or take the risks necessary to tap our full potential.

Amusement.

We become amused when something unexpected happens that makes us laugh. This amusement or laughter is "heartfelt" and accompanied by a

---

66. *Finding the Midline*, at 144.

67. *Positivity*, at 44–45 (describing the value of pride).

68. *Finding the Midline*, at 144 (describing when pride can get away from us and is no longer an asset).

desire to share the fun. Such experiences offer the chance to build relationships with others.[69]

Generally, the type of amusement I discuss here requires that it be experienced in a social gathering and that it arises in a safe setting as opposed to the type of nervous laughter we might experience when we are scared.[70] While laughter in and of itself, even in private, is healthy and beneficial, **the sharing of laughter optimizes amusement as an element of wellbeing.**

Fortunately, I can think of any number of examples in which I have experienced the positive emotion of shared amusement. Recall my friend Jim, the one who suggested I give yoga a try years ago. We stay in touch by phone all the time, even though we live across country from each other. One reason I make it a point to talk to him regularly is that he makes me laugh. I never know what he is going to say that is funny or when he will insert humor into the conversation or even a text message. But I know he will. Who doesn't appreciate a friend like that?

We know from the last chapter that the development of positive relationships is one of the five elements of wellbeing. As much as we must be serious in the face of life's daily challenges, it is important to remember the value of sharing humor as a way to open the door to new relationships.

Inspiration.

We feel inspired when we come across excellence, catching a glimpse of human potential, even our own. Our innate desire to fully understand and express ourselves is stimulated and we feel the urge to try to excel. Our passion to be the best version of ourselves is ignited.[71]

---

69. *Positivity*, at 45 (commenting that "amusement is social" and so laughing in solitude pales in comparison to shared laughter).

70. *Positivity*, at 45.

71. *Positivity*, at 44-45.

For a great example, consider the inspiring story of an American paratrooper who developed serious back and knee problems from making so many jumps during the Gulf War. He was told he would never walk without crutches. Believing that to be the case, he did nothing by way of even routine physical activity, using crutches and even a wheelchair to get around. After years of inactivity he became seriously overweight.

Eventually, his personal pride caused him to say "enough." When he was 47, he learned about a yoga workout he could do at home and he began a steady practice, with guidance from the teacher who created the workout program. This war veteran's transformation is amazing. After diligently following the yoga program, falling down and getting up over and over again, he eventually developed significant strength and balance, and slimmed down to a very healthy weight. Most amazing of all, not only could he walk without crutches, he could actually run with ease.

While the story is inspiring in and of itself, what is even more inspiring is the YouTube video of his transformation.[72] In the video we initially see him in a wheel chair, dependent on family and friends to take him places. Because he videotaped his progress, we watch him at first unable to do even the most basic yoga poses without falling down and requiring chairs to stand back up. He falls on his face, crashes into furniture, and faces challenges that would cause many of us to quit. But he keeps going. As the video progresses, we get to watch fantastic change take place as we see his tremendous willpower at play.

In the end of the video he doesn't even look like the same person. Every time I watch the video my eyes well up with tears and I feel the power of transformation in me. I forget my own little problems. I feel inspired. I haven't just watched his transformation, I've watched what is possible, in some form or another, for me. **As we go about our efforts to build a life of wellbeing, we may from time to time pause as we ponder what we might do to be meaningful in some way.** A great "go-to" answer to that question is to follow the inspirational example of this war veteran and strive to be

---

72. This footnote directs you to a YouTube video "Never, ever, give up. Arthur's inspirational transformation!" This is a video of Gulf War veteran Arthur Boorman. https://www.youtube.com/watch?feature=player_embedded&v=qX9FSZJu448; retrieved June 19, 2018.

the best we can be. Whatever it is we are doing, there's a good chance somebody will notice and be inspired by our passion.

Awe.

We experience awe when we encounter something astonishing. We feel reverential, struck with wonder as we stop and attempt to take in the sheer magnificence of what we are seeing. Humbled, we try to assimilate the magnitude of what has caught our attention.[73]

We may have felt this way when we saw the Grand Canyon or some similar wonder of nature. We might feel this way when we witness a breathtaking athletic performance, hear a brilliant piece of music played by a master, or even eat a particularly well prepared, innovative meal.[74]

Opportunities to feel this sense of awe arise more often than we might think. We don't have to visit the Grand Canyon or buy tickets each week to some event. We simply need to tune in our attention to the wonder of human ingenuity and endeavor. For example, I remember how awestruck I was after listening to my friend's description of a surgery she had undergone. It was a highly invasive surgery required in response to unexplained pain in her midsection. As the doctors performed the surgery through a very tiny insertion into her body, they used gas to gently separate tissue to investigate what was happening. With a tiny light, they found a very serious, unexpected medical condition, and were able to successfully treat it.[75]

When she told me about the surgery, I was blown away by the brilliance of those who were able to create such devices and procedures. The world is really full of wonder, not only as expressions of nature but also through the expression of human potential.

---

73. *Positivity*, at 46–47.

74. *Positivity*, at 46–47 (providing examples of situations evoking awe).

75. *Finding the Midline*, at 222–223.

We all have stories of how we've been struck with wonder at something nature offers us, whether a sunrise, a sunset, the wind, the rain, a soft breeze, or a beautiful meadow. Similarly, maybe we have been amazed at a ridiculous athletic move, a dance performance, a rendition of a song, or other human feats, such as the engineering genius of a tunnel through the Rocky Mountains or how a computer works. **To help build wellbeing, we simply have to be awake to all the wonder around us.**

Love.

We normally think of love in terms of a romantic relationship or the feelings we have for our family, even our pets. I am going to share with you a description of love that is different and might surprise you.

The love we consider as one of the ten most common "positive emotions" can exist in any number of forms or relationships. This love is the feeling that arises when we experience and share any of the other positive emotions we've been discussing in the context of a safe interaction with others.[76] Examples include the sharing of our hopes and dreams with another or the serenity of being part of a strong relationship.[77] It can include the shared laughter I described earlier or the mutual feeling of joy the NFL football players experienced in their spontaneous touchdown celebration.

When we share any of these positive emotions, there is a potential for those persons sharing the emotion to experience what is called a "positivity resonance."[78] A positivity resonance occurs when the sharing of a positive emotion produces a "momentary upwelling" of emotion attributed to a vibratory synchronization of two or more person's biochemistry and behavior.

---

76. *Positivity*, at 47.

77. *Positivity*, at 47 (providing examples of the positive emotion of love).

78. Fredrickson, Dr. Barbara (2014 ed). *Love 2.0.* New York, NY: Penguin Group (USA) LLC., at 17 (introducing the phrase "positivity resonance" as a "shorthand" explanation for what she refers to as the positive emotion of "love").

This synchronicity then results in each person feeling a warm connection to the others and a desire to invest in each other's wellbeing.[79]

These moments of resonance can be momentary and are not exclusive with just one other person. They don't have to occur with a special friend; they can even occur with strangers.[80] This positivity resonance, this "connection," is the positive emotion of love.[81]

When we view love this way, we see that we've experienced love, positivity resonance, with others outside of a romantic relationship. We've shared laughter with friends and felt the warmth of the connection we feel with those friends in that moment. Or, as part of a team we've felt pride in each other when we've won a big game or championship. We've quite possibly shared moments of awe or interest with friends while traveling or out for an evening, seeing a rainbow or listening to a good band.

We've also probably experienced positivity resonance with strangers. I remember going to a Boston Red Sox baseball game at Fenway Park with my son. The Red Sox were in the running for a pennant and every game mattered. The Sox trailed the Minnesota Twins heading into the eighth inning but tied the game up and, with two outs, they took a one run lead. Fans in the stand were cheering wildly and I remember at least one guy I didn't know turning to me and giving me a big "high five."

The Twins came to bat in the ninth and, with one out, put runners on second and third base, representing the tying and winning runs. I looked around, and not a single person was sitting. Everybody was yelling as loud as they could at the Twins' batter, each of us looking knowingly at each other with the shared conviction that we could yell loud enough to make him strike out. And, at least on that night, it worked. The Red Sox held on to win. People hugged each other, and thousands of people left the

---

79. *Love 2.0*, at 17.

80. *Love 2.0*, at 16–17 (describing that the love she references is not "exclusive" to spouse, partner, family, and close friends but, rather, refers to the bond we create with whomever we've connected).

81. *Love 2.0*, at 16–17 (stating that when we resonate with another in this way, we experience an "ability to see others," giving us a "sense of oneness and connection, a transcendence that makes you feel part of something far larger than yourself").

stadium, happily resonating with the shared joy of this come from behind victory.

Part of the process of awakening to our full potential is to awaken to the opportunities life offers us to experience positive emotion. If there is the possibility of laughter, joy, or inspiration inside us, that's part of our potential too. To ignore our emotions or shortchange them is to miss part of the experience of being alive. **Our potential isn't measured only by successfully concluding a challenging task. It is also measured by successfully awakening to and embracing the highest potential of each moment, whether that experience be one of joy, gratitude, pride, wonder, or any other positive emotion.**

Chapter 3
Engagement

Engagement refers to those times when we get lost in an activity of our own choosing. We become so totally focused and absorbed on our task that we lose track of everything else.[82] Our thoughts and emotions merge with the object of our attention.[83] Self-consciousness disappears, and time seems to stop. We don't want whatever it is that has so captivated us to end.[84]

There are many examples of engagement. A few include: participating in sports such as tennis or a pick-up basketball game; playing card or board games; learning something new, like a language, a musical instrument, or a martial art; working on projects for our job; making music; drawing; sculpting; getting immersed in a scientific analysis; reading a book; rock climbing; dancing; sightseeing; and sailing.[85]

Let's look at rock climbing as an example of engagement. Rock climbing demands that we pay full attention to what we are doing in every single moment. It challenges a climber's strength, stamina, balance, and agility. In addition, it tests the climber's mental discipline because it requires full focus. One simple mistake can result in injury or even death not only for the climber, but also for his or her partner or others. There is no room for getting mentally sidetracked worrying about something else, like work, the bills, or what to eat for dinner. With such complete concentration, the climber becomes totally absorbed in the details of the ascent to the

---

82. *Flourish*, at 16–17 (describing engagement to include the experience of time appearing to stop and we lose all sense of self-consciousness).

83. *Flourish*, at 11; 16–17 (reporting that engagement results in a complete absorption in the task).

84. *Authentic Happiness*, at 114.

85. Csikszentmihalyi, Dr. Mihaly (2008 ed.). *Flow*. New York, NY: HarperCollins Publishers (describing throughout the many types of activities that can lead to engagement).

exclusion of everything else. And climbers will tell you that they can spend hours during a strenuous and challenging climb, and it seems like only minutes. This is engagement.

Engagement can be more, though, than just a short-term respite from our daily grind. People who learn to make engagement a regular part of their life tend to transform themselves over time into more confident, powerful people. They do this by repeatedly choosing to undertake activities that push them to greater levels of performance and self-awareness. By doing so they continually become more and more complex, expanding their "self."[86] This is the very essence of what I've been talking about so far; the ongoing, expansive cycle of discovering our potential, developing it, and then expressing it. We did ten pullups yesterday, let's do eleven today. We climbed a 5.5 rated route last week, let's go for 5.6. This is our human nature.

How is it possible that engagement can lead to greater self-awareness and expand the self? Certainly not every engaging activity accomplishes this objective. To maximally experience these transformative benefits of engagement we need to be selective in our choice of activity. That said, what factors are present when a person is fully engaged in a transformative activity?

The factors of engagement.[87]

First, the activity must have a clear goal. There must be a well-defined purpose for the activity and the steps required to complete it. We know what we are trying to accomplish and how to proceed. Using our rock-climbing example, there is typically a clearly-defined end point for the climb, with the objective of getting from the bottom to the end point.

---

86. *Flow*, at 74 (reporting how increasingly complex, challenging activities that push a person to a higher level of performance transform the self).

87. These factors come from: Czikszentmihaly, Dr. Mihaly (2013 ed). *Creativity*. New York, NY: HarperCollins Publishers, at 110–113. (listing and description of nine factors).

Next, the activity must provide immediate feedback. During each step of the way we know whether we are on the right track or not.

For an activity to have potential to transform us as a person, it has to challenge our skills but not be too overwhelming. The activity must be challenging enough to test us, but not so overwhelming that we constantly feel the "anxiety" of being in over our head.[88] These feelings of anxiety create the very type of self-consciousness that interrupts full engagement. Further, if our skills aren't up to the task to begin with, we will become increasingly frustrated when we continually fail to develop competency in the activity.

It is the matching of our skills to the challenge that makes an activity potentially transformative for us, potentially leading us to that higher state of consciousness I mentioned previously. This is how that transformation happens. Over a period of time, as we continue to engage in a particular activity, we move through a learning curve. With appropriate practice we get better. Eventually, what once was exhilarating and challenging about that activity may even become boring as we master the task. Having mastered the activity, we then move on to a new challenge, armed with increased self-confidence by our success. We've expanded our understanding of who we are and what we might be capable of doing. We've redefined "the best version of ourselves" and we want to keep upping the ante, expressing our central need of affirming ourselves as a person "of worth and dignity."[89]

From time to time we may find that an activity isn't a good match for our skill set. We realize that we are overmatched. This, too, is part of expanding our self-awareness as we become better able to appreciate our own set of strengths and talents even as we accept our limitations. There is a freedom that comes from understanding that we can't be good at everything, that it is impossible. Knowing this, we feel liberated in a sense, allowing us to find a different activity that is more suitable for us.[90] At the

---

88. *Creativity*, at 111.

89. *The Discovery of Being*, at 80 (stating that self-affirmation is a central need); *Man's Search for Himself*, at 96 (referencing our need as human beings to feel we are someone of "worth and dignity").

90. *Flow*, at 75 (stating that the frustration of being overmatched in an activity can

same time, we save time and energy by looking to others to handle tasks we know aren't our forte. As one of my yoga philosophy teachers likes to say: "Sanskrit is tough. It might be a good idea for your own emotional stability to leave the translations to me, just like I leave the lawyering to Dorigan over there, engine tuning to Peter, or wine selection to Laura (a Master Sommelier)."

Another factor present with engagement is **we pay full attention** to what we are doing. We aren't multi-tasking. We have a single-pointed focus.[91] Think again of the rock-climbers who can ill-afford to be thinking about problems at work while they are 100 feet above the ground on a sheer rock face.

When we are engaged, we don't get distracted. The "intense concentration" on the task at hand acts like a barrier to prevent distractions arising from stray thoughts unnecessary to complete the task. Thoughts or things going on around us that might normally cause us to ruminate or distract us are unable to break through the barrier of our total concentration.

During times of engagement failure is not a concern. We have a reasonable expectation that we can handle the challenge. Once we step into the challenge by undertaking the task, our concentration is so complete that we aren't processing thoughts such as failure.

Engaging activities cause us to lose self-consciousness. Our focus on the activity is so absolute that our ego has nobody to listen to it. We have no attention available to spend on concerns such as what others might be thinking of us or what type of impression we are making.

I think of times as a young lawyer when I was playing pickup basketball at the Minneapolis YMCA. There were some really good players, including several current (at that time) and past Minnesota Viking football players who were not only highly tuned athletes, but also huge; 6'5' and

---

stimulate us to find a new way to use our skills in a more satisfying manner).

91. *Creativity*, at 111–112 (reporting that when a person is fully engaged, their attention and the activity "merge" due to the one-pointed attentiveness required because of the "close match between challenges and skills") .

240, 6'7" and 305. I was 5'11" and 168. These lunch-time games also included others who had played basketball in college. My talent level didn't come close to the talent on the court, but when it was my turn to play, I had a great time, doing what I could do well in that situation: run around to get open, look for a good pass to make, take an open shot when it was within my range, or hustle to at least be a minor irritant defensively to whomever I was guarding. I was so engaged in the game that I didn't think about how much better all these other players were than me. I didn't wonder what they thought of me. My ego stayed on the bench. And, thankfully, none of them ever treated me like I didn't belong.

In situations of engagement we lose any sense of time. During these games the lunch hour flew by, I was enjoying myself so much.

Yet another factor that indicates full engagement is that the activity is the end in itself. We do the activity for its own sake, as opposed to attaining some other goal. Each pickup basketball game I played in continued until one team reached a certain score. Then, teams were shuffled as players waiting to play switched with one or two players who had been playing the longest, even if those players were on the "winning" team. Those players voluntarily relinquished their spot on the floor because that was the way it was done. During a lunch hour there might be five or six games, one after another. There was no set "team" that stayed together from day to day, or even over any single lunch hour. Unlike a regular basketball league, there was no way to win any trophy or award. The only goal for any of us was playing basketball.

Regardless of which activities we choose, times of engagement can be the best moments of our lives.[92] While engaged we feel powerfully in control of our actions, unburdened by the usual chatter of conflicting thoughts racing through our mind, such as whether to remodel the kitchen, or how do we get the neighbor to change the paint color on his or her house? [93] Our total focus liberates us from such distractions, making us

---

92. *Flow*, at 3 (describing that our best moments usually occur when our "body or mind is stretched to its limits in a voluntary effort to accomplish something difficult and worthwhile").

93. *Flow*, at 23–42 (discussing the processes by which we grow the self).

feel like we are "masters of our own fate," free to stretch ourselves to the limit physically or mentally.[94]

When we become engaged in an activity of our own choosing, we break out of the prison of unwanted and potentially debilitating negative thoughts and feelings. Life loses its ability to play games with our mind as if our thoughts were a steel ball in a pinball game, being flipped forcefully from bumper to bumper and over and around ramps by somebody other than us. **In contrast, total engagement causes us to feel truly alive and in charge of our life as we tap in to our primal urge to fully express ourselves.**

Learning how to direct our attention.

An essential skill for experiencing more engagement in our life, and, there-fore, more wellbeing, is to master how we direct our attention.[95] By developing greater awareness of what is happening around us, we are better able to recognize and choose engaging activities that appeal to us. By learning how to better direct our attention we become more adept at noticing how we feel in different circumstances. This is how we develop preferences; i.e., "I like writing stories;" "I really enjoy downhill skiing;" or "I love cooking and entertaining." Also, by learning to pay attention we discover what we don't like, what we prefer not to repeat too often, if at all.[96]

We store all these preferences as memories. When we combine our memories with greater awareness, including self-awareness, we are better able to shape future experiences, creating a life of our choosing. How does this happen? First, we see opportunities to become engaged in activities that suit our preferences, while steering away from things, as best we can, that we would prefer not to do. In this way, we begin to guide our choices

---

94. *Flow*, at 3.

95. *Flow*, at 30–33 (stating that the ability to focus our attention at will and without distraction until we achieve our task, is a "priceless resource"); *see also Aware*, at 4–5 (identifying focused awareness as essential to wellbeing).

96. *Flow*, at 31.

of action so as to repeat favorable experiences as often as possible.[97] As much as our social and work obligations allow, we make choices with our free time that honor our preferences, at the same time staying away from those things we would prefer not to do, if we can help it, that drain our time and energy. We develop a lifestyle in which we choose activities that engage us and that will best improve the quality of our life.[98] This is a part of what I mean by "mastery" over our mind.

Mastery over our thoughts and feelings leads to a richer life, a life filled, as best we can, with activities that engage us. We become such a master not only by maximizing use of our free time to engage in activities that honor our preferences, but also trying when possible to direct our work life in the same way. **A "secret to a happy life" is to find a way to be totally engaged in as many of our required daily activities as possible, as, for example, a professional musician who loves playing and also gets paid for it.**[99]

Developing the skill of awareness, along with the ability to sustain focus, are major reasons why practicing and studying yoga is so transformative. Yoga teaches us the skill of increasing our awareness of what is happening around us in every moment, and then the skill of maintaining our concentration on that which we choose to pursue. In fact, yoga is considered "one of the oldest and most systematic methods" of producing the experience of engagement.[100] In Part 2 I explain how yoga practices, including the eight limbs of yoga taught by the yoga sage Patañjali approximately 2,000 years ago in his *Yoga Sūtras*, are a literal roadmap for showing us how to develop the mental clarity and focus we need to create wellbeing in our lives.[101] Patañjali's *Yoga Sūtras* are considered by some to

---

97. *Flow*, at 34–36 (describing the process of becoming master of our experiences).

98. *Flow*, at 33.

99. *Creativity*, at 113 (discussing how an activity can become autotelic, meaning that we do the activity for the experience of doing it, rather than in furtherance of a particular end).

100. *Flow*, at 103–106.

101. The date of Patañjali's *Yoga Sūtras* is a subject of debate, with some scholars dating this work to just after the turn of the Common Era, between 100 and 200 C.E.; Bryant, Dr. Edwin (2009). *The Yoga Sūtras of Patañjali*. New York, NY: North Point Press, at xxxiv.

be the bible of yoga[102] and respected as one of the most important texts in Hinduism and a classic of world thought.[103] Believed to be a compilation of yogic philosophy and practices up to the time they were written, they cover "centuries of lively experimentation and thought about the great matter of self-transcendence."[104] Guiding us step by step through these limbs, Patañjali teaches us about the clarity and focus required for meditation, describing meditation as the means for achieving the ultimate goal of yoga, total absorption or connection with the object of our attention. (I discuss meditation in detail in Chapter 9.)

Notice how the objectives of full engagement and yoga are the same, total absorption of the self with an activity of choice. In yoga this total absorption is called Samādhi, and is described by yoga expert B.K.S. Iyengar as follows:

> Uninterrupted flow of attention dissolves the split between the object seen and the seer who sees it. Consciousness appears to have ceased, and to have reached a state of silence. It is devoid of 'I', and merges into the core of the being in a profound state of serenity. In *samādhi*, awareness of place vanishes and one ceases to experience space and time.[105]

Whether we seek to establish more engagement and wellbeing in our life or, instead, to find *samādhi* in a meditation practice, the ability to direct our attention through greater awareness and focus is key. With greater awareness we pay closer attention to our preferences as well as the opportunities life provides that match well with them. We then are in a

---

Other scholars date the text much earlier, between 500 and 200 B.C.; Iyengar, B.K.S. (2002 ed). *Light on the Yoga Sūtras of Patañjali*. London, ENG: Thorsons, at 1.

102. *Light on the Yoga Sūtras of Patañjali*, at viii.

103. *The Yoga Sūtras of Patañjali*, at xviii.

104. *The Yoga Tradition*, at 198 (writing: "For the student of Yoga, it is important to know that Patañjali's *Yoga-Sūtra* was preceded by centuries of lively experimentation and thought about the great matter of self-transcendence.... [It] "scarcely betokens the immense ingenuity and spiritual creativity on which it was built").

105. *Light on the Yoga Sūtras of Patañjali*, at 181 (commenting on Patañjali's *Yoga Sūtra* III.3).

better position to make choices that we know will engage us or otherwise further wellbeing. Next, through application of the skill of sustained focus, we can follow through on our choices with the uninterrupted flow of attention needed for success.

Identifying our strengths.

An optimal way for choosing which opportunities for engagement to pursue is to take on challenging tasks that require application of what positive psychology refers to as our "highest strengths." These strengths are our internal qualities, "most deeply characteristic of us," that best describe who we are at our essence, our most authentic self.[106] Research has identified twenty-four character strengths: appreciation of beauty and excellence, bravery, creativity, curiosity, fairness, forgiveness, gratitude, honesty, hope, humility, humor, judgment, kindness, leadership, love, love of learning, perseverance, perspective, prudence, self-regulation, social intelligence, spirituality, teamwork, and zeal.[107]

There is an important distinction between our character strengths as used in this context, and skills or talents we might have, such as "perfect pitch" or the body and speed of a long-distance runner.[108] For example, I was skilled at taking depositions as a trial attorney. Professional musicians

---

106. *Authentic Happiness*, at 13; 38.

107. This list is provided by the VIA Institute on Character, a non-profit organization "dedicated to bringing the science of character strengths to the world through supporting research, creating and validating surveys of character, and developing practical tools for individuals and practitioners." The list of strengths is based on work directed by Dr. Martin Seligman and the late Dr. Christopher Peterson, Professor of Psychology at the University of Michigan, and validated by Robert McGrath, Ph.D., Professor and School Director at Fairleigh Dickenson University, Teaneck, New Jersey. See Peterson, Dr. Christopher and Seligman, Dr. Martin (2004). *Character Strengths and Virtues: A Handbook and Classification*. New York, NY: Oxford University Press, Inc. These strengths are associated with a set of core virtues that can be developed through these strengths. For further information, visit the Institute's website: http://www.viacharacter.org/www/Character; retrieved December 10, 2018.

108. *Authentic Happiness*, at 134.

are talented or skilled at playing their particular instrument.[109] In contrast, we also have character strengths of the type I refer to here. I've learned that one of my character strengths is creativity. This strength helps me design innovative yoga class themes that can entertain and inspire the students. It is no surprise, then, that I find satisfaction teaching yoga classes. To fully develop our potential, we need to be aware of both our talents and skills, on the one hand, as well as our particular character strengths on the other.

To maximize wellbeing, we want to tap into every bit of what we have to offer, our entire range of abilities as well as what drives us. When we recognize these character strengths, these deep, internal qualities we possess, and employ them in whatever activity we select, we tend to excel, feel excited and invigorated, powerful, and we experience a creative joy.[110] This is particularly the case when we match up these character strengths with tasks that challenge us. This matching of strengths with a challenge is what creates an environment for experiencing high levels of full engagement.[111]

To assist us in identifying our top character strengths, you can do what I did—take a free online evaluation. This online evaluation, which takes under a half hour, can be reached through the link on the website identified in this footnote.[112] You'll be given your results online. After getting your results I suggest reading what the website has to say but also consult Chapter 9 of Dr. Seligman's book *Authentic Happiness* to obtain guidance on how to interpret and use your results.[113] Identifying our highest character strengths is of tremendous help to us in creating a life of wellbeing by

---

109. I distinguish the two terms "talent" and "skill" as follows: A talent is something we are born with, an ability to do something, whereas a skill is something we work to develop and express. For further discussion of this distinction, see the discussion under the subsection "Attaining goals" in Chapter 5, and the underlying resource cited, Duckworth, Dr. Angela (2016). *Grit*. New York, NY: Scribner, at 33–51.

110. *Flourish*, at 38–39. *See also Authentic Happiness*, at 160 (identifying indicia to help determine which strengths on the list are one of your highest or "signature" strengths; this indicia includes feelings such as a sense of ownership ["this is the real me"], a sense of yearning to find a way to use the strength, and an ease of using the strength).

111. *Flourish*, at 24.

112. This link is directed to the website for the VIA Institute on Character. http://www.viacharacter.org/www/Character-Strengths-Survey; retrieved June 20, 2018.

113. *Authentic Happiness*, at 134–260.

showing us how to best express ourselves each day in a way that causes us to feel most alive and passionate. Living this way leads to a life of "abundant gratification and authentic happiness."[114] The survey is a tremendous gift to us for that purpose, helping guide us in our choices of activities to pursue.

114. *Authentic Happiness,* at 161.

Chapter 4
Meaning

As humans we need a purpose. We want our life to account for something, to have some meaning. To live a life rich in meaning and purpose, what is called in positive psychology "the good life," we need to identify our skills, talents, and strengths and share them in service of something bigger than ourselves. [115]

The human drive to find meaning in life has long been recognized. For example, in his best-selling book, *Man's Search for Meaning*, first published in 1946, psychiatrist Viktor Frankl describes how he was able to find meaning even through his experience in a Nazi concentration camp during World War II. He described the brutal, cruel daily struggles during his captivity and how he sought to find a way to keep going, to find a purpose for survival, a reason for living.

From this experience, which included losing his entire family to the gas chambers, Dr. Frankl concluded that finding meaning is "the primary motivation" in a person's life.[116] He wrote that it is up to us to examine what we have to offer, to identify our unique experiences, strengths, and abilities, and then determine how the world can benefit from what we have to offer.[117] We need to be on the lookout for those "assignments" life gives us that demand fulfillment.[118] This is how we can find meaning because

---

115. *Flourish*, at 17; *see also Authentic Happiness*, at 260.

116. Frankl, Dr. Viktor (2006 ed). *Man's Search for Meaning*. Boston, MA: Beacon Press, at 105 (disputing those who contend meaning is just a "secondary rationalization," stating that meaning is "unique and specific").

117. *Man's Search for Meaning*, at 113–116.

118. *Man's Search for Meaning*, at 113 (stating that the meaning of life differs for each of us, with each of us having our own unique role to play, a "concrete assignment" or "mission" which gives us a specific meaning in life).

meaning is derived from looking outside ourselves, "to something, or someone, other than oneself."[119]

Opportunities to experience meaning appear regularly.[120] We can create or experience meaning in at least these four ways: 1) through our own creative work or actions; 2) by recognizing meaning when it presents itself to us; 3) through our interactions with others; and 4) through our attitude when we confront suffering; i.e., we can choose to find meaning in adversity.[121] Let's take a closer look at these various options for creating or experiencing meaning.

Creating meaning through our work and actions.

How do we create meaning through our work or actions? Whenever we create something, we actualize or affirm ourselves, causing the sense of satisfaction I've mentioned earlier.[122] When we create something for others to consider and perhaps enjoy, such as work created by poets, artists, scientists, musicians, writers, teachers, and inventors, we feel a glow of creative self-expression by service to others.[123]

We don't have to write poetry or create significant works to share with the public, like a painting or a cure for a disease, in order to create meaning. I found meaning as a trial lawyer working on cases that helped people.

119. *Man's Search for Meaning*, at 115.

120. *Man's Search for Meaning*, at 115 (suggesting that the "more one forgets himself—by giving himself to a cause to serve or another person to love—the more human he is and the more he actualizes himself").

121. *Man's Search for Meaning*, at 115.

122. May, Dr. Rollo (1975). *The Courage to Create*. New York, NY: W.W. Norton & Company, Inc., at 39–40; 134; 140 (discussing ways to create meaning). For other resources on creating a meaningful life, consider: Dalai Lama (2002). *How to Practice: The Way to a Meaningful Life*. New York, NY: Pocket Books; Tolle. Ekhart (2005). *A New Earth: Awakening to Your Life's Purpose*. New York, NY: Penguin Group, and Cope, Stephen (2012). *The Great Work of Your Life: A Guide for the Journey to Your True Calling*. New York, NY: Bantam Books, to name just a few.

123. *The Courage to Create*, at 39–40.

But even before I became a lawyer, I found meaning working behind the counter at a downtown, busy department store treating people with respect and kindness. Not everybody that stepped up to the counter was in a good mood or having a great day. They were often harried and clearly under stress. I challenged myself to be especially nice to such people, particularly those who seemed grouchy, to see if I could get them to smile or maybe even laugh.

If we have a job that brings us in contact with the public, rest assured that there will be times when we are the only kind voice somebody hears that day, or the only person who makes eye contact and smiles, the only person who listens. Even if we don't work with the public, I'm hard pressed to think of a job that doesn't provide a needed service to somebody. We create meaning for ourselves simply by doing our job competently and with integrity and basic kindness, making sure the service we're employed to provide is dependable and provided in an honest way. We can take pride in making sure that the fruits of our labor are worthy of the hard-earned dollars somebody chooses to pay for them.

We can make a difference with our actions in any number of ways other than through our occupation. We learn to pay attention to life and listen when circumstances ask something of us. For example, my Denver friends Chris and Lisa work hard during the week at their respective jobs, but still found time during a crisis to volunteer at a Catholic Charities center to help victims displaced by a huge fire. Their desire to be meaningful to their community prompted them to be of service. My neighbor Jeff is a retired Air Force colonel and has plenty to do even in retirement from the military. Still, he finds time to respond to fire and emergency calls as a Captain of our volunteer fire department and also as an EMT on the town's "FAST (First Aid Stabilization Team) Squad" set up to respond to 911 calls in our rural area to help victims until the paramedics arrive.[124] Knowing these people, I can see where they've found a way to use their character strengths, whether kindness, bravery, or other strengths, in service of something bigger than themselves. They are each living the good life, a life of meaning and wellbeing.

---

124. *Finding the Midline*, at 75 (pointing out that we "don't have to be grandiose about it;" we can be creative by looking for a way to serve a purpose for our family, our community, or society in general).

As my examples illustrate, society offers many structures, such as churches and various volunteer organizations, which provide opportunities for us to be of service. Some of these opportunities require some level of talent, training, or experience, but others only need our willingness to sacrifice free time. Societal structures offering chances to meaningfully contribute to our community include participation in politics, volunteering at church, working for causes such as the environment, community activities, family services, schools, and youth sports, among others.[125]

One of my most treasured memories is of the three years I volunteered as an assistant ice hockey coach for my son's high school team. As a coach, opportunities to share what I'd learned playing high school and college sports, participating in martial arts competitions, as well as working in the business world as a lawyer, were constant. For example, one young sophomore shared with me that he felt ashamed because he didn't like getting hit hard during the practices or games. This was his first experience at the high school level, and the amount of intense checking was far greater than what he had experienced in junior high school. When I told him that "nobody likes getting smacked," and that "I never liked it," all the way through college football, it was like a breath of fresh air and dignity for him. He decided to take his lumps, if necessary, and play. He ended up on the varsity and was a solid contributor all the way through high school. Also, as he grew both in size and confidence, he in time became a pretty scary guy to play against if you were from another high school. He went from being afraid of being hit to being one of the hardest checking players on the ice. He also grew into a very self-assured young man off the ice. This was a young man who for whatever reason felt like opening up a bit to a coach but not with his parents. All I had to do was listen. Being the coach was a perfect vehicle for creating some meaning in my life through sharing my background and strengths with somebody else. I feel I made a difference for him and that makes me proud, even today, well over twenty-five years later. It was my memory of this meaningful time in my life that prompted me to consider teaching yoga as a way of finding more life satisfaction while working as a lawyer.

---

125. *Flourish*, at 12.

Finding meaning when it is presented to us.

Additional ways of finding meaning in our life is by encountering something that moves us. For example, we can experience meaning when we witness acts of goodness or honesty, or when we come across beauty, nature, and culture.[126] We explored this idea in our discussion of positive emotion, as, for example, when we discussed the value of feeling in awe of something or being inspired. Rather than creating meaning for others, these experiences are meaningful to us because we are touched deeply in ways that cause us to feel the wonders of being alive. When I visited Machu Picchu in Peru I was stunned to silence by the ruins. I experienced a similar reaction when I took a tour of the Anne Frank museum in Amsterdam, captured by the reality of all that this attic represented. In both cases I had to sit down and take time to contemplate and assimilate the experience.

Dr. Frankl provided a very touching example of being moved by nature and circumstance in a meaningful way. He described a scene just days after being liberated from the prison camp. Emotionally numb, suspecting (correctly) that his wife and children had been gassed to death and that his world had been torn away from him, he went for a walk through a meadow. The winter was over, and the meadow was filled with fragrant and colorful wild flowers waving gently in the breeze, accompanied by the soft chirping of some larks. Overwhelmed, he fell to his knees in prayer. After some time, he stood up, knowing that he was now ready to start over again with life. His moment in that meadow was incredibly cathartic: "Step for step, I progressed until I again became a human being."[127] His experience of beauty in the meadow allowed him to again find meaning in his life.

This ability to experience meaning from something outside us is fundamental to our wellbeing. Our capacity to be awake to life's invitations is a foundational necessity to creating a life of wellbeing. Being aware in each moment opens the door to experiencing and sharing a positive emotion, finding engaging activities, spotting opportunities to help others, identifying worthy goals for ourselves, or creating and nurturing positive relationships. For Dr. Frankl, I suspect that by falling to his knees in prayer

---

126. *Man's Search for Meaning*, at 115.

127. *Man's Search for Meaning*, at 95–97.

in that place and at that moment, he opened his badly wounded heart to a powerful, healing sense of life's potential and how he could serve that potential by helping others.

Finding meaning in our interactions with others.

Another way of creating meaning is through our interactions with other people. In fact, this can be a profound and wonderful way to increase meaning in our life. We do this by truly experiencing another person. We don't just learn the basics about that person, such as their name, where they live, their job, and how many kids they have. We go much, much deeper. We set aside any agenda other than truly knowing this person.

Employing the tool of empathetic listening we discussed in the last chapter, we gradually become fully aware of the very essence of that person, their experiences, abilities and highest strengths. We search for and uncover that person's full potential. Then, having done this, we act like a mirror for that person, reflecting back to them all that they are capable of being. And, we don't stop there. We then help them manifest their newly discovered potential.[128] In this way we create meaning not only by helping another discover and express himself or herself, but also, by this unveiling we make available to the world that person's previously undiscovered potential as he or she begins to express it.

We very briefly discussed the yoga concept of *samādhi*, total absorption, in the last chapter on engagement. It is worth mentioning again here. As I'll explain further in Chapters 9, in his *Yoga Sūtras* Patañjali goes to great lengths to describe the process of ever deepening levels of meditative absorption, stages which develop within the practitioner the ability to experience and even eventually merge with the essence of the object of meditation, *samādhi*.[129] In Patañjali's yoga, that object is the individual soul.

---

128. *Man's Search for Meaning*, at 116 (writing that through love we can enable another to "actualize" their potential).

129. *The Yoga Sūtras of Patañjali*, at 61–79; 142–168 (commentary on Patañjali's *Yoga Sūtras* 1.17–22 and 1.41–1.51, describing different levels of absorption, *samādhi*).

Patañjali's description of these increasingly subtle levels of *samādhi* are a beautiful and highly useful template for showing us how we might meaningfully and fully engage with another human being. We do so by following the process of empathetic listening I described above. When we invest in a person in this manner, becoming fully engaged in such an intimate connection with that person, we've created meaning. We've brought into the light the full power of a person where otherwise that power would have remained at least somewhat hidden in the dark, dormant and wasted. For this reason, among many others, Patañjali's *Yoga Sūtras* are a tremendous tool for helping us build wellbeing. I'll return to them throughout this book.

Finding meaning in suffering.

We can also create meaning in our life by looking for meaning in the midst of unfortunate events or suffering, including hopeless situations, those times when "fate...cannot be changed."[130] In any difficult predicament we can challenge ourselves to change our attitude in response to the problem confronting us, rather than allowing ourselves to be overwhelmed and lost in despair. We do this by looking for some value or lesson in the situation, trying to find meaning in our life.[131]

I recall a yoga retreat in which one young woman who had recently lost her mother broke down during a session, overcome by her grief. The teacher listened to her and, at the right moment softly told her how blessed we all were to get to know the greatness of her mother through knowing this young woman at the retreat. I wish I could remember his exact words, so perfectly stated, but the point of sharing this story is that the teacher gave this woman a sense of purpose in the midst of her sadness. She could honor her mother by being the wise, graceful, kind woman her mother had been.

---

130. *Man's Search for Meaning*, at 116.

131. *Man's Search for Meaning*, at 116–117 (suggesting that "man's main concern is not to gain pleasure or to avoid pain but rather to see a meaning in his life").

Maslow's Hierarchy of Needs as a guide for meaning.

As we search for additional ways to find or create meaning in our life, we can also consider Dr. Abraham Maslow's "Hierarchy of Needs."[132] Dr. Maslow identified five categories of human motivation:

1. physiological needs (basic needs for survival, such as water, food, shelter, clothing, sex);

2. safety needs (stability, freedom from fear, the need for law and structure, job security, health);

3. belonging and love needs (family, friendships, intimate sexual relationship);

4. esteem needs (confidence, self-respect, a desire for mastery and achievement, prestige, status, fame); and

5. self-actualization needs (the need to be true to our own nature, doing what we are "fitted to do," a desire to be everything we can be).[133]

While this hierarchy is typically depicted as a pyramid, with physiological needs at the bottom and self-actualization at the top, human beings can experience needs from different levels in any order and in combination.

We can use this hierarchy of needs as a guide for how to direct our efforts to find meaningful ways to be of service. For example, if we contribute to our neighborhood food shelf, we are helping others meet their

---

132. Maslow, Dr. Abraham H (1970 ed). *Motivation and Personality*. New York, NY: Harper & Row, Publishers, Inc. Later in his career Maslow identified another level of meaning beyond self-actualization—"self-transcendence." *See, generally,* Maslow, Dr. Abraham H. (1971). *The Farther Reaches of Human Nature*. New York, NY: Penguin Books, at 259–286 (describing the ability to set aside our own needs and concerns to serve something bigger than ourselves, as, for example, putting aside our personal situation in order to serve values such as truth, beauty, goodness, justice, and even joy or playfulness; at 128–129; 262).

133. *See, generally, Motivation and Personality*, at 35–46.

most basic physiological needs for survival. Or, like my neighbor, when we volunteer for training and service on our local First Aid Stabilization Team or fire department, we contribute to needs for safety.

With respect to helping others fulfill the need for belonging and love, there are many ways to reach out to family and friends to express love and friendship. We can take time to call a family member or friend just to let them know we are thinking about them. I can't express how good it makes me feel when one of my friends from Colorado call me just to "check in." And, although we talk often, I most appreciate when my son calls just to see how I'm doing.

We can even "create" family and friends by finding a group dedicated to something we care about, like maintaining hiking trails, presenting community music events like my friend, Ron, does, or any number of other activities. In this way we provide a meaningful service to others whose needs include love and feelings of connection to others. And by doing so we also help meet our own need for the same.

We can pay attention in the workplace for opportunities to help others feel a sense of self-esteem, confidence, and self-respect. Such chances exist if we look for them. For example, I had a senior partner to whom I reported when I practiced in a large, national law firm. One time, during a firm-wide partners' meeting, with partners present from all over the country, he stood to tell all the partners about a fantastic result we'd achieved for a major client. Instead of simply telling the firm about the result, he made it a point to give me a lion's share of the credit. For some of these partners this was their first real introduction to me and their first direct impression of my value to them as a younger partner. Talk about building my self-esteem and confidence!

Going back to ice hockey, I remember my son's college coach taking my son aside after a game and telling him: "If you keep playing like that, you'll be a force to reckon with in this conference." I think my son's feet (or skates) didn't "touch the ground" for a month and his play reached a new, higher level as his confidence soared.

I suspect that in a typical work environment it would be possible to find an opportunity most days, with full sincerity, to help build somebody's confidence or sense of self. And a parent or partner can do wonders by taking time out to look for a way to honor their family members by acknowledging them in an appropriate way.

Finally, at the top of the Maslow pyramid, we have the ability to focus, from time to time, on another person in order to help that person awaken to his or her own potency and then manifest it. In this way we serve another in helping them meet their need for self-actualization.[134]

---

134. Maslow identified behaviors leading to self-actualization, including total absorption, making choices as part of a pattern of personal growth, letting our true self emerge, taking responsibility, and "actualizing one's potentialities at any time, in any amount," among others. *The Farther Reaches of Human Nature*, at 40–49.

Chapter 5
Accomplishment

Accomplishment involves setting and achieving goals.[135] Not every accomplishment need be achievement of a life goal in order to increase our wellbeing. Accomplishments include reaching whatever goals we pursue, of our own free will, just because we feel like it.[136] Think back to our rock-climbers. Safely summiting a challenging rock formation on a Saturday afternoon is clearly an accomplishment. Just as running your first marathon, landing a dream job, winning a ribbon at the state fair, or being elevated to "First violin" in the orchestra are all accomplishments. So, too are winning a hand of bridge, finally weeding the garden, or organizing a closet.

Life changing or not, each of these are accomplishments that contribute to our wellbeing. This is the case because our human nature is to "exert mastery over the environment."[137] If we choose to pursue an objective, whether coming in first in a race or winning a game of chess, and we succeed, that is an accomplishment that adds to wellbeing. It nourishes our desire to express our potential in some fashion.

We set goals and undertake to achieve those goals for a wide range of reasons. Some achievements are tied to a greater purpose or meaning, but many are not. Some of us want to build a deck, transform a basement, or finally clean out the inside of our car. Accomplishment as an element of wellbeing pertains to successfully completing whatever task we choose to undertake solely because we want to.

---

135. *Flourish*, at 110 (pointing out that the farther away the goal is from the starting point, "the greater the achievement").

136. *Flourish*, at 20.

137. *Flourish*, at 18–20.

Winning is a key aspect of this element of wellbeing. Examples include pursuit of wealth for no reason other than to accumulate more than others, playing a game purely to win, and building a business to make it the largest of its kind.[138] While many people do meaningful service through their wealth or businesses, this service is only a "side effect" of their efforts; their true motivation is to succeed, to win.[139]

There is a reason accomplishment, the desire to win, is included as an element of wellbeing. As I mentioned in Chapter 1, **an underpinning of Dr. Seligman's wellbeing theory is that it is a "theory of uncoerced choice," meaning each of the five elements are things people choose to undertake for their own sake, rather than to gain any other objective.**[140] We choose to laugh and enjoy a positive emotion because we desire such experiences. We select projects that engage us because that is how we wish to spend our time, lost in an activity, free from our everyday chattering patterns of thought. There are times we wish to help family, friends, or our community, so we choose of our own volition to do something meaningful, whether it is volunteering to rid our local roads of clutter or helping collect clothing for the needy. We opt to spend time with certain people because we enjoy being in relationship with them. These are our choices.

This free choice of how to spend our time, effort, and resources is an underpinning of the element of accomplishment. Winning, successfully accomplishing things, is a driving force of human behavior. As humans, we desire "accomplishment for the sake of accomplishment."[141] We seek to achieve success in the fields of our choice.[142] It is for these reasons that it is included as one of the five elements of wellbeing.[143]

---

138. *Flourish*, at 18–19 (providing examples of undertakings pursued for their own sake).

139. *Flourish*, at 19.

140. *Flourish*, at 16.

141. *Flourish*, at 19 (commenting that including accomplishment as an element of wellbeing is not an endorsement of a life directed to winning but, rather, to point out that this is one of the things "human beings, when free to choose, select "for its own sake").

142. *Flourish*, at 20.

143. *Flourish*, at 14–20 (stating that the task of positive psychology is to describe, not prescribe, what people do to achieve wellbeing).

The desire to win is so strong that it can be easy to get attached to the "achieving life,"[144] a life spent flitting about pursuing unrelated and, many times, short-term objectives. We are wired to seek success, to take on challenges because it feels good to win. **Unfortunately, without cultivation of the other elements of wellbeing, such a life focused only on achievements minimizes the level of wellbeing we will develop in our life.**[145] Remember, wellbeing is measured in total by how much of each of the five elements we manage to include in our life. How much positive emotion, engagement, meaning, accomplishment, and positive relationships do we cumulatively enjoy?[146] Although the desire to achieve is a basic human drive, it is only one of the five that constitute wellbeing.

To self-indulgently focus only on accomplishing a myriad of goals without regard to the other elements of wellbeing can lead to a lonely end, I suspect. We end up much like Ebenezer Scrooge, the Dickens character in "A Christmas Carol," prior to his ghostly visits. Scrooge was a wealthy miser, isolated by choice, who experienced few positive emotions, and did little by way of creating meaning or enjoying positive relationships in his life, despite his affluence. Fortunately, the ghosts of positive psychology visited him in time for him to make a change. As the book (and movie) ends, Scrooge has seen the light, giving a huge tip to a young lad to go buy a large turkey to bring to the Cratchit family, followed shortly thereafter by agreeing to take care of Tiny Tim's health issues. These acts brought meaning to his life. We see Scrooge experiencing positive emotions as he joyfully dines with his nephew's family, having previously rejected their invitations for years. At the dinner he begins to forge relationships with family members that he will carry with him into his now bright future. We leave him building a life of wellbeing where, before, he was a sad, forlorn, angry but very accomplished rich guy. He is no longer the lonely, cranky miser sitting on his accumulated wealth.

As this Christmas classic demonstrates, in order to fill our life with wellbeing, we must learn how to accommodate our innate desire to achieve

144. *Flourish*, at 20.

145. *Flow*, at 214 (suggesting, for example, that if we don't link our activities in a meaningful way, we will remain "vulnerable to the vagaries of chaos").

146. *Flourish*, at 15; 20.

while at the same time pursuing opportunities to fill our life with the other four elements of wellbeing. To do this, we must become selective about what goals we choose to pursue. After selecting a worthy goal, we must be efficient in how we direct our efforts towards achieving it. Only then can we more fully attain wellbeing, a life filled not only with accomplishments, but also with positive emotion, engagement, meaning, and relationships.

Choosing goals.

How do we learn to become more selective in what goals we choose to pursue? One way is to identify our strengths, as we discussed in Chapter 3. Great satisfaction in life comes from finding, developing, and using our strengths.[147] So, in selecting goals to pursue, we try to find activities that use our strengths. We also, of course, look for activities that are engaging, that challenge us but aren't so far beyond our capacity that we will become frustrated and quit.[148] We will find more satisfaction pursuing those goals that challenge us but are, with proper effort, attainable.[149] Of course, as we develop our potential by successfully reaching the more challenging goals, we raise the bar, so to speak, as goals that at one time seemed out of the question start to appear on the horizon.

When considering what goals to pursue, we ask ourselves what interests us, what do we feel passionate about. We are far more likely to find overall satisfaction if, in choosing our goals, we devote our strengths towards something that we find not only engaging but also something that arouses our passion.[150] In determining how to direct our energies, we learn to stop and ask ourselves basic questions, including how we like to spend our time, what do we daydream about, and what is important to us.[151] Once

---

147. *Authentic Happiness*, at 13; 260.

148. *Creativity*, at 111 (stating that true engagement requires that our abilities are "well matched" to the challenge).

149. *Flow*, at 72-77.

150. *Grit*, at 95–116 (discussing greater job satisfaction associated with doing something that comports with our personal interests).

151. *Grit*, at 114–115 (suggesting ways to identify our passions).

we recognize our interests and our passions, we use that information as a life compass, keeping us on track towards selecting and attaining those goals that further those interests and passions.[152]

One tool to help establish a set of goals and then stay on track towards attaining them is to create a "goal hierarchy."[153] We use a goal hierarchy to clarify our goals, identifying not only long-term goals, but also short-term goals that serve as stepping stones. Such a goal hierarchy helps us avoid other tempting activities that are not compatible with or, even worse, conflict with the ultimate goal.[154]

Let me give an example of how we can sometimes get in our own way when we are pursuing a goal and why a goal hierarchy is so helpful. I remember years ago when I was working very hard to pass my first black belt exam in Shotokan Karate. As you can imagine, the work included kicking which, in turn, required flexible legs with fast-twitch muscle action. In other words, my legs needed to move fast. At the same time, I decided to train to run a marathon, a 26-mile race. The training for the marathon required a large amount of slow distance running, not very helpful for improving my fast-twitch muscle action in the legs.

One day my karate teacher, Sensei, pointed out to me that I was working at odds with myself, developing tighter, slower legs from running while at the same time I was trying to do the opposite to qualify to take my black belt exam. Not only that, the daily long training runs took time away from karate training. For example, I skipped Saturday morning karate classes, a class in which Sensei devoted time to helping students prepare for their belt exams, so that I could do a longer run with my running group. I was clearly getting in my own way if I wanted a black belt. And, not only was I interfering with my karate goal, all the difficult karate training during the week tired me out, taking away from my marathon training.

---

152. *Grit*, at 60.

153. *Grit*, at 64-66 (describing a goal hierarchy).

154. *Grit*, at 64–78 (offering suggestions on how to make a goal hierarchy effective).

Sensei first asked me why I wanted to run the marathon and my answer was two-fold: first, because it would be an accomplishment; and second, because I liked the social camaraderie. Cardiovascular fitness was a relative wash; both karate and running did that to the degree I was concerned about.[155]

We then discussed why I wanted a black belt in karate, and I had a much more nuanced set of reasons. Like yoga, karate teaches us the self-awareness needed to relax the tension that contributes to tighter, slower muscle action. For example, if I went to karate class all stressed out from a deposition, the muscular tension fueled by my higher stress levels slowed down my blocks, punches, and other techniques. The chest, shoulders, and arms simply can't move as quickly when they are tense. In karate, as I later did with yoga, I worked on my stress from the outside of my body inwards by first recognizing which parts of my body were holding tension and then asking them to relax so that I could punch, block, and kick more quickly. This necessarily involved identifying underlying thoughts and emotions that were contributing to the muscle tension. Through this process of self-inquiry, I learned to recognize the causes of my tightness and then, having done so, better relax and release tension in my muscles. Further, by having also identified the underlying sources of mental anxiety leading to the physical tightness, I was able to work on dealing with those issues. The results of this process carried over into work activities, such as depositions or at trial. In addition, I learned to release tension more readily at social engagements, driving in crowded traffic, and virtually everywhere else. I knew I wanted to be a more relaxed, "easy to be around" guy, and karate, by helping me identify the sources of my stress, and then relax, was changing me into a more pleasant person to be with. That transformation was a priority goal for me, and achieving that goal was my passion.

That conversation with my teacher helped me figure out which activity, training for a karate black belt or completing a marathon, was more

---

155. Certainly, running and karate training are different in terms of developing cardiovascular conditioning. During the time period I discuss in the text I was in excellent cardiovascular shape and, for my particular purposes, refining that condition during that time period wasn't a concern for me. My primary reason for wanting to run a marathon was for the purpose of accomplishing a new goal; i.e., completing a marathon—another "feather in my cap," albeit a very worthy objective.

important to me at that time. I decided to go for my black belt, and thus achieve the underlying benefits I so much wanted in addition, of course, to the big accomplishment of earning a black belt. I decided I could train for another marathon later. As for social interaction with the running group, Sensei laughed and then pointed out I could come to karate class on Saturday morning and then join the group for breakfast at the end of their long 20-mile run, the timing of which worked out perfectly. The rest of the week I could do a few short runs with the group at lunch, as we always did, and then use the other weekly run times to practice karate and stretch.

And that is how it turned out. I passed my exam, got my black belt, and later, over the next few years, completed a few marathons as well. I maintained my relationships with the running group while I trained for my black belt and was even invited to their post-race party.[156] Although, it could be they invited me because they wanted protection.

Attaining goals.

Once we set our priorities, it still takes persistent effort to achieve our goals. Although talent is helpful, without effort, talent "is nothing more than your unmet potential."[157] To become skillful in whatever endeavor we undertake, to fully develop our potential, we must apply effort in the use of our talent. Then, it takes ongoing, consistent effort to refine our skills until we accomplish our objective, reach our goal.[158]

I had no particular level of talent when I first walked into the karate dojo as a brand-new beginner. While I had participated in sports my whole life, those sports had, if anything, made me stiffer and tighter than other

---

156. For another resource discussing how to identify what is most important to us and avoiding the distractions that get in the way of achieving goals, *see* Fritz, Robert (1989 ed.) *The Path of Least Resistance. Learning to Become the Creative Force in your Own Life.* New York, NY: Ballantine Books.

157. *Grit*, at 51.

158. *Grit*, at 35–51 (describing how we must first apply effort to our talents in order to become skilled, then in order to achieve a worthwhile goal we must continue to apply effort through use of that skill).

people who had never played football or trained with weights. Through long training under the guiding eye of my teachers and senior students, I slowly developed skills such as kicking, punching, blocking, and, most importantly, avoiding kicks and punches thrown my way. By the time I was a purple belt, I had some pretty good skills. However, there is a big difference between a purple belt and a black belt, and it took many, many more hours of ongoing, consistent effort to cultivate my skills to the point where I was able to pass a black belt exam.

High achievers learn to cultivate their efforts through forming habits of focused, deliberate practice.[159] They seek feedback on what they are doing right and also wrong.[160] Then, after assimilating that feedback through consistent, proper practice, such achievers learn to let go, and practice without judging their efforts because those judgments can derail them.[161]

For example, in karate classes Sensei watched every move we made, stepping in as needed, which could be quite often or sometimes not at all, to suggest refinements. For me he at first had to remind me pretty regularly to relax my neck and shoulder muscles so that they didn't take energy and power away from my body movements. I'd take a breath, quell my frustration, and then release the tension and continue. Over many hours of practice, with Sensei there to remind me, I lost the habit of tensing my neck, giving my body more freedom to move as the situation demanded. Had I not been able to accept his coaching and "let go" of this habit, and the attitudes that led to that habit, I would have remained a brown belt. And, I would have continued to go through life carrying excess stress, with no ability to let it go.

Not surprisingly, yoga also emphasizes practice as a necessity for accomplishing our goals. The goals of yoga are accomplished through

---

159. *Grit*, at 131; 137–140. For an excellent resource on how to develop helpful habits and eliminate habits that don't serve us, *see* Duhigg, Charles (2014 ed). *The Power of Habit*. New York, NY: Random House.

160. *Grit*, at 121–123.

161. *Grit*, at 140–142 (explaining how to get the most out of practice, we must, without judging ourselves, be able to pay close attention in each moment for the feedback from the practice we need to calibrate our efforts).

"practice" (*abhyāsa*)[162] performed properly, without interruption, and over a long period of time in order for a skill to become firmly established.[163] Such practice must be performed with "dispassion" (*vairāgya*), without anxiety about the final result.[164]

Recognizing our accomplishments.

Once we achieve a goal, recognizing our accomplishments is a vital practice for creating wellbeing. When we pursue a goal and achieve it, we have an opportunity to use the accomplishment as a way to build our sense of self.[165] We can pause and reflect on our successful completion of a task and, by doing so, add to our self-esteem and confidence.[166] By pausing to savor our achievement, we develop a sense of justifiable pride, one of the positive emotions we discussed in Chapter 2.[167]

I find that pausing to reflect with pride when I attain a goal is a healthy, even vital action for increasing my wellbeing. By recognizing my achievements, I feel stronger, and better able to tackle something new, even something I would not previously have thought attainable for me. My horizons expand and broaden after every success. My sense of confidence grows. By acknowledging my success at achieving one thing, I become inclined to reach even higher or into a whole new arena of endeavor. For example, one day I decided I was tired of looking at a broken rail on my deck. I figured out what was needed, bought the materials (and the tools) and fixed the railing. This was something I normally wouldn't have tried

---

162. *The Yoga Sūtras of Patañjali*, at 43–47 (commenting on Patañjali's *Yoga Sūtra* 1.12).

163. *The Yoga Sūtras of Patañjali*, at 49–51 (commenting on Patañjali's *Yoga Sūtra* 1.14).

164. *The Yoga Sūtras of Patañjali*, at 51–57 (commenting on Patañjali's *Yoga Sūtra* 1.15)

165. This link is directed to the following article: Soots, Lynn, "PERMA—A is for Accomplishment/Achievement." *The Positive Psychology People* www.thepositivepsychologypeople.com/perma-a-is-for-accomplishment/; retrieved March 11, 2018.

166. "Perma—A is for Accomplishment; *citing* Bryant, Dr. Fred and Veroff, Dr. Joseph (2007). Savoring: A New Model of Positive Experience. Mahwah, NJ: Lawrence Erlbaum Associates, Inc., at 5.

167. *Positivity*, at 44–45.

to do myself. I stood back, admired my work and swelled with pride. "Look at what I just did!" I sat there on the deck for a while, savoring my accomplishment.

Next, feeling good about myself, I picked up the phone and called a friend of mine, invited her over, and together we made a plan to re-do the entire landscaping in my backyard to go with the freshly repaired deck. I'd not done much landscaping before but, what the heck, if I could do the deck repair, I could certainly rip up the whole yard and transform it into a mini-national park. Such is the power that comes from taking time to savor our accomplishments.

Chapter 6
Positive Relationships

We require relationship with other people in order to fully experience well-being. The most enjoyable and meaningful things in our lives occur with others, seldom alone.[168] For example, pride in our accomplishments is most satisfying when shared.[169] In addition, we need relationship with others to make our way in the world and even to ensure our very survival. Our brains are programmed to work socially with others to solve common problems, allowing us each an opportunity to survive and hopefully flourish.[170]

Let's explore the role of positive relationships as an element of wellbeing, as well as the idea that our brains are actually wired to connect with others.

Relationships for increasing wellbeing

It's Sunday night, Super Bowl night in February 2016, and I'm at home in Vermont watching the Denver Broncos in a hard-fought battle with the Carolina Panthers. I'm not only a football fan but also a big Bronco fan. Although I've moved from Colorado to Vermont, my loyalty remains with the Broncos. Unfortunately, it's hard to find Bronco fans around here, particularly with Tom Brady's success with the New England Patriots. So,

---

168. *Flourish*, at 20 (stating that "[V]ery little in life that is positive is solitary," using as examples, feelings of indescribable joy, profound meaning, and pride. "Other people are the best anecdote to the downs of life and the single most reliable up").

169. *Flourish*, at 20.

170. *Flourish*, at 21–24 (suggesting that the human brain evolved in the way it did in part to help us be social problem solvers. This allows us to better get along with others and build relationships to help insure our survival as a species, much like hive behavior of wasps, bees, and other insects).

with no family around this evening, I'm watching the game alone, with my dogs around me who are apparently uninterested in the result.

Even though it's been years since I've played in college, football means a lot to me. I spent years, from junior high school through college, working hard to make the teams and get to play. Some of my closest friends are guys I played with. There's a special bond that is forged by teammates. I imagine that this type of bond is not unique to sports, but this is what I know from my own experience. I think, down deep, many of us when we played in high school, and then in college, dreamed of being a pro and playing in the Super Bowl. While I long ago waved goodbye to the dream of a pro career, the imprint of those memories must remain because when the big game arrives, I'm excited. And when my favorite team is in the game, I feel an energy running through me that is tough to explain except for that imprint.

The Broncos and Panthers scratched, stomped, and clawed, and the game was up for grabs late in the fourth quarter, with the Broncos clinging to a very tenuous six-point lead. Then, with just over three minutes left, the Bronco's C.J. Anderson punched in a touchdown and Payton Manning threw a pass for a two-point conversion. This gave the Broncos some breathing room and they held on to win, 24-10. I was thrilled, way too thrilled to savor the win alone. But I was alone, except for the dogs who continued to be unimpressed. Although, one of them looked up to see why I was jumping up and down and yelling while I pumped my fists in the air in celebration.

Actually, though, I wasn't alone. I knew my good friend Jim, back in Colorado, the guy who introduced me to yoga, had also been watching the game and was no doubt jumping up and down in his living room just like I was. I was bursting with the desire to share the moment with somebody, particularly a friend I knew would be every bit as excited. I picked up the phone and called him. He answered and off we went in a shared celebration of our Bronco moment. The victory was made sweeter sharing it with my buddy on the other end of the phone call.

I have plenty of these types of stories about sharing a special moment and I suspect you do as well. **Life's experiences seem richer when they are shared with others.**[171] Research shows we are "biologically programmed" to place importance on interaction with others. According to social scientists, people claim to be most happy when they are in the company of other people.[172] In fact, one of the surest ways to get out of a funk and get a "hit" of wellbeing is to follow the advice of the bumper sticker: engage in a "random act of kindness." Such acts are the "single most reliable" way to provide a momentary increase in wellbeing.[173]

There is some highly regarded, well-funded, long term research to support the claim that positive relationships are critical to wellbeing. The Harvard Study of Adult Development (originally called the Grant Study), has been ongoing for over seventy-five years. The study tracks the lives of certain individuals, including a group of college men, as they age, in an attempt to identify the conditions that promote optimal health. The Chief Investigator for the study from 1972 to 2004, Dr. George Vaillant, published his impressions of the study's key results in a 2012 book entitled *Triumphs of Experience*.[174]

Dr. Vaillant described how the study focused on ten later life accomplishments, the "Decathlon of Flourishing," representing many different variables of success.[175] Accomplishments on the list included being listed in

---

171. *Flourish*, at 20.

172. *Flow*, at 164–165 (reporting that social science surveys "universally" conclude that people say the company of others boosts happiness).

173. *Flourish*, at 20.

174. Vaillant, Dr. George E. (2012). *Triumphs of Experience*. Cambridge, MA: The Belknap Press of Harvard University Press.

175. *Triumphs of Experience*, at 29–31 (identifying the ten variables of success, which they called the Decathlon of Flourishing: 1) inclusion in "Who's Who in America; 2) earning in the top quartile; 3) low in psychological distress; 4) success in work, love, and play after age 65; 5) physically active after age 75; 6) good physical and mental health at age 80; 7) master of the Eriksonian task of Generativity (a measure of whether a person is engaging in meaningful activity); 8) availability of social supports other than wife and kids between ages 60 and 75; 9) in a good marriage between the ages of 60 and 85; and 10) close to kids between ages 60 and 72.

Who's Who in America, income levels, and relationships with others.[176] The study followed the subjects to determine which of the variables mattered most in their later years in terms of wellbeing.

Based on the results, Dr. Vaillant concluded that "the most important influence by far on a flourishing life is love. Not early love exclusively, and not necessarily romantic love…Happiness is love."[177] While early love in childhood is important, he found from the study that with nurturing relationships later on in life we can lead a long, rich life of wellbeing: "Childhood need be neither destiny nor doom."[178]

If happiness is love, where does the love come from? Dr. Vaillant wrote that **our relationships shape our lives** and that "the most important contributor to joy and success in adult life is love (or, in theoretical terms, *attachment*.)"[179] Love in this context is the positivity resonance of shared experience with others that we discussed in Chapter 2; it is the emotional feeling of connection.[180]

When I was able to share my excitement over the Bronco Super Bowl win with my friend, I was experiencing the type of nurturing happiness that the Harvard Study is finding to be so important to wellbeing. That is just one example of how relationships help increase the satisfaction of our life experience. Think of how much more satisfying it is when you watch a good movie, whether comedy or drama, with somebody you like. The comedy scenes seem funnier and the drama feels like it touches us more deeply. And, this will sound familiar to some of you, I can't describe how quickly my mood improves when I answer my phone and hear "Hi Grandpa!"

---

176. *Triumphs of Experience*, at 27-53 (describing conclusions as of the date of publication, 2012, including: 1) having love in life is the "most important influence by far on a flourishing life;" 2) people can change and grow; and 3) we "are shaped and enriched by the sustaining surround of our relationships").

177. *Triumphs of Experience*, at 52.

178. *Triumphs of Experience*, at 52.

179. *Triumphs of Experience*, at 52; 369–370 (emphasis in original).

180. *Love 2.0*, at 17 (describing the momentary upwelling that constitutes love as consisting of the convergence of sharing a positive emotion between people, a synchrony between them of their biochemistry and behaviors, and a reflected motive to invest in each other's wellbeing and mutual care).

The connection we feel in these shared experiences of positivity reso-nance can lead to a mutual desire to invest in each other's wellbeing and, as I discussed in Chapter 2, can even occur with strangers. How does this happen? Developments in neural science confirm that we are in fact wired to connect with each other. Mirror neurons allow us to literally share our emotions with another through various ways such as our facial expressions and body language.[181] Two brains can create a "functional link, a feedback loop that crosses the skin-and-skull barrier between bodies."[182] This feed-back loop puts us in synch with the other person, allowing us to feel what they are feeling.[183]

Because of this power of connection, it is important that we choose our company wisely. The company we keep can make life either very rich or "utterly miserable."[184] My teacher, Dr. Douglas Brooks, reminds us, **"we become the company we keep, so keep great company."**[185] We want people in our lives that nurture us, show us our potential in a way we can't see for ourselves, and then support us as we strive to grow into that potential.

We can enrich our lives not only by taking care of those relationships we already have, but also by opening our minds to the potential for new and interesting relationships, including with people different from us. Getting to know people different from us is a key to fully appreciating life. Such people offer us new perspective and viewpoints. They expose us to ideas that we might not otherwise consider. **People who are different from us are not threats to who we are; they are clues to what we can become.**[186]

181. Goleman, Dr. Daniel (2006). *Social Intelligence*. New York, NY: Bantam Dell, at 41–43 (explaining how mirror neurons "reflect back an action we observe in someone else, making us mimic that action or have the impulse to do so").

182. *Social Intelligence*, at 39–40 (describing how two brains couple, with the output of one brain becoming the input for driving the workings of the other brain, creating a temporary interbrain circuit).

183. *Social Intelligence*, at 42.

184. *Flow*, at 164.

185. Brooks, Dr. Douglas R. Public Lecture. Howard, Colorado. July 14, 2011.

186. Brooks, Dr. Douglas R. Public Lecture. Howard, Colorado. July 14, 2011; *and see Finding the Midline*, at 79–81 (discussing the potential that exists in relationships, in-cluding people with whom we are unfamiliar because it is within the unknown that the greatest possibilities exist).

Through interaction with the unfamiliar we expand who we are, what we know, and, thus, what we have to offer.

We also can enrich our lives by tending to those relationships we already have. We can devote energy to better know our friends, workmates, and family. When we are with them, we can engage in the process of empathetic listening, listening in order to more fully understand them and to remember their preferences. Through such listening we can add meaning to these relationships, serving as a nurturing mirror for them, showing them what we've learned about them that they may not know. In doing so we help them be all they can be.[187] These are the kind of friends we want in our life, so we can start by being that kind of friend ourselves.

Relationships for survival

As I mentioned at the beginning of this chapter, we also need relationships with others to help each other get along and survive in the world.[188] Think about what we take for granted in our daily lives. For most of us, much of what we rely on each day involves somebody else doing their job. For example, we likely use roads, somebody had to build and maintain them. We rely on fire and police protection, as well as the safety of a strong military. When the power goes out, we rely on the utility company. If we are sick, or our pets are sick, we rely on trained professionals to help with healing.

At the store, we assume the clerks and staff keep the shelves stocked with what we want. We wear clothes somebody designed and made. Our food itself, with few exceptions, comes from the efforts of others, not only the producers of the food, but also those who transport it, those who price it, and those who sell it. Even if we live off the grid, somebody else probably made our solar panels, helped us drill our well, or fabricated the containers we use to catch river or rain water.

---

187. *Man's Search for Meaning*, at 116.

188. *Flourish*, at 21-24.

The list of ways we depend on each other is endless. Everything in our lives that helps us survive and thrive requires the assistance, usually unseen, of others. We're part of that web of service as well. Whatever it is we do for a living, or as a volunteer, helps others in the course of their day.

One of the things that makes me proud to live in my small Vermont town is attending the annual "Town Meeting" and watching our town folk each year interact at these meetings. Year after year we agree to spend our hard-earned dollars to support programs like Meals on Wheels that help keep people alive who we often don't even know. One year we might vote to pay for a new fire truck so that, collectively, we can protect the people and property in the town and be a responsible member of a collective of neighboring town fire departments that help each other. At a recent meeting, we voted for a new grader for the road crew. Fortunately, this wasn't the same year we agreed to buy the fire truck!

At the Town Meeting we agree to fund road repairs so that our neighbors can get to where they need to go and be serviced by fire, police, and ambulance, even though we don't know everybody else or even where some of the roads are located. We help pay for other resources in adjacent towns, such as the great library and the senior activity center in nearby Montpelier, nature trails, parks, and all sorts of things, some of which we ourselves never use. We do it because we recognize we are part of an interdependent community.

It's a bit hard to leave at the end of Town Meeting without feeling proud. I think that is the case because at our core we are good, benevolent people who feel honored and gratified to be able to take care of each other. Also, though, it is because we know subconsciously that we need to take care of each other to survive. Intuitively, we understand that "what goes around, comes around." That person who couldn't get to the hospital because the road wasn't plowed could be me. The elderly woman who starved because she had no social support and no Meals on Wheels could be our parent, it could be us someday. The next house that burns to the ground because we voted down the request to buy a needed tanker truck could be ours.

I bring up Town Meeting because when we are able to consider issues locally and without the craziness of big-time politics, we know deep down what is right when it comes to helping each other out. We know deep down, that we are wired to serve each other.[189] **We need the social fabric of friends, and groups, whether family, neighbors, or a community, to take care of ourselves in time of need.[190] We need each other to thrive as human beings.**

---

189. *Flourish*, at 22–24.

190. *Flourish*, at 23.

Chapter 7
Emotional resilience

To build wellbeing we must also understand and develop emotional resilience.[191] Emotional resilience is the ability to live our lives successfully and happily notwithstanding the "stress or adversity" that can otherwise get in our way.[192] It is the way we respond and deal with obstacles life puts in our path, including those we create ourselves. No matter who we are, there will be times when our best laid plans are challenged by any number of things including what other people say or do. And our own patterns of viewing ourselves and the world will challenge us. How we respond is a measure of our emotional resilience. Recognizing this process and then developing emotional resilience will directly impact how much wellbeing we are able to build in our life.

An example of emotional resilience.

We don't know what adversity will come our way or when it will appear. I know of a yoga teacher, well-loved by her students and friends, a great mom and wife. She was vigorous, athletic, and seemed to be in great health. One day, though, she was diagnosed with cancer and had to undergo chemo and

---

191. There are at least four categories of resilience: 1) physical resilience, the body's ability to recover from illness or injury; 2) cognitive resilience, the ability to remain focused in the face of stress; 3) emotional resilience, the ability to experience positive emotions and bounce back quickly from negative emotions; and 4) spiritual resilience, the ability to maintain our values and commitment to something bigger than ourselves in the face of adversity. Sood, Dr. Amit (2015). *The Mayo Clinic Handbook for Happiness*. Boston, MA: Da Capo Press, at 38–39.

192. Cyrulnik, Dr. Boris (2011 ed.) *Resilience*. London, ENG: The Penguin Group, at 5. *See also The Resilience Factor*, at 11–12.

other treatments people with cancer have to endure. Instead of allowing herself to be swallowed by sadness, fear, anger, or frustration, she kept a positive attitude. She continued as best she could to teach her classes, wearing a scarf over her head when she lost her hair. During that time, when she fought to heal and wasn't sure if she was winning that fight, she gave some of the finest, most inspiring classes she'd ever taught.

A friend of mine who attended her classes told me that she became a true inspiration. She was a model of character, grace, and dignity while struggling through the disease and the heart-breaking ups and downs of her treatment process, including the effects of the treatments. Her response to her illness, her resilience in dealing with its challenges, motivated my friend to elevate his own way of showing up in the world.

When we are faced with challenges and even disaster, we can curl up in a ball, try to hide, become overwhelmed with anger, or any number of other defensive responses. We can withdraw into a shell like a turtle and try to avoid any further disruption in our lives. But, doing so will cost us. It will cost us in terms of making us "numb" to all the good that life offers, including the experience of warm relationships, more positive emotion, chances for engagement, invitations to offer our gifts in service or as inspiration, and pride in our accomplishments.[193] Such reactions also rob us of any learning experience that the challenge presents. In other words, the failure to develop and be able to call upon emotional resilience will cost us our wellbeing. The yoga teacher I described has healed and even now uses her experience as an inspiration for others.

Our deeply held attitudes and beliefs about people can also impede our ability to experience and build wellbeing. Such attitudes and beliefs run the gamut from feelings about race, other cultures, other religions, gender preferences, or any distinction that are part of what makes people so special. Many of us also have unresolved personal issues including fear, anger, lack of confidence, and other limiting beliefs about ourselves. All of these attitudes and beliefs can limit our ability to recognize and pursue invitations to greater wellbeing because we will either avoid or refuse to

---

193. Love 2.0, at 77–78 (describing emotionally resilient people as generally being "emotionally agile," able to deal with adversity by an appropriate emotional response, "neither overblown nor insensitive").

engage in situations that challenge these attitudes and beliefs.[194] **To build a life of wellbeing, we have to identify our patterns of potentially limiting attitudes and beliefs and confront them as they arise.** Otherwise, many of life's opportunities for building wellbeing, such as experiencing more positive emotion or developing new, interesting relationships, will slip through our fingers.

Developing emotional resilience.

If emotional resilience is so important, how do we develop it? A "lucky few" of us are born with emotional resilience.[195] Others learn resilience through good parenting. However, even if we missed the boat on DNA or ideal parenting, research confirms that emotional resilience "can be acquired."[196] **The "number-one roadblock to resilience" is the way we view the world and interpret what is going on around us.[197] Our unique style of thinking, the way we interpret our experiences, "bias and color our viewpoint," creating the self-defeating attitudes and beliefs I mentioned.**[198] We develop these patterns starting at an early age and they impact how we interpret and respond to life's opportunities as well as its challenges.

---

194. For a discussion of how our belief systems can lead us away from reality and sabotage wellbeing, consider Festinger, Leon (1962 ed). *A Theory of Cognitive Dissonance.* Stanford, CA: Stanford University Press, at 260–266 (describing in detail the author's theory that humans seek internal harmony and consistency in their opinions, attitudes, knowledge, and values. This is consonance. When a fact arises that is dissonant, inconsistent with the person's belief system, that fact threatens to disrupt that harmony. This can result in mental pressure to find a way to interpret that new fact in a way that returns the person to mental harmony; i.e., consonant).

195. *Positivity*, at 110.

196. *Learned Optimism*, at 29–30.

197. *The Resilience Factor*, at 11. The authors of the *The Resilience Factor* are Drs. Karen Reivich and Andrew Shatte. Dr. Reivich is the Director of Training Programs at the Penn Positive Psychology Center and Dr. Shatte is the founder and President of the Phoenix Life Academy, a training company focused on measuring and training for resilience, and is a Research Professor at the University of Arizona Medical School. Both are psychologists specializing in helping people develop resilience and their book serves as a guidebook in developing such resilience in ourselves.

198. *The Resilience Factor*, at 12.

The great news, though, is that we can learn to overcome these self-limiting ways of viewing life.[199] Consider, for example, the potentially debilitating condition referred to as "learned helplessness.[200] Learned helplessness is a pattern of thinking that allows life's challenges to wear down certain people and they simply give up trying. Even when opportunity presents itself, learned helplessness can cause such people to feel so out of control of their destiny that they forgo the chance to better their condition. To overcome self-defeating patterns of attitudes and beliefs, including learned helplessness, we can begin to view life through the prism of what is referred to as "learned optimism:" "Each of us carries a word in his heart" that shapes how we view what happens in our lives: either a "no" or a "yes."[201] We can teach ourselves to access the "yes," much like the yoga teacher I wrote about earlier who, in the face of cancer, said "yes" to continuing to live a meaningful life.

We can develop the habit of saying yes to life by learning to recognize every unhelpful attitude and belief that arises, challenge them, and then replace them with "an optimistic personal dialogue."[202] Sometimes this process can include the consideration of alternative explanations to the negative patterns that, if left, unchecked, can lead to self-destructive behavior.[203] For example, I had a history of trying to be perfect at whatever I do; an attitude that, if left unchecked, drove me bonkers because, near as I can tell, it's impossible to be perfect at much of anything. To combat my tendency of getting down on myself when I struggled with a task, I learned to stop and remind myself that not everybody can be good at everything and that I'm really good at certain things, just not this particular thing I'm trying to do.

---

199. *Learned Optimism*, at 16–30 (discussing Dr. Seligman's work demonstrating that resilience can be acquired).

200. *Learned Optimism*, at 17–30.

201. *Learned Optimism*, at 16.

202. *Learned Optimism*, at 90–91 (describing how skills learned in cognitive therapy can help people change habits they use in times of adversity) .

203. *Learned Optimism*, at 89–91 (explaining tactics used in cognitive therapy).

I use that system today to help me stay optimistic and confident. For example, when my car needs some work, I remind myself that car repair isn't my thing. To get me back into a "yes" frame of mind towards life, I remind myself that I'm really good at other things, such as taking depositions in a lawsuit as well as providing much needed humor when the occasion requires it. This little bit of personal dialogue helps me to avoid going down the rabbit hole of self-disdain. I don't give a negative personal dialogue a chance to take over; it's immediately challenged and replaced with an optimistic perspective on myself.[204]

Another way to build our emotional resilience is through the use of what is called the "broaden and build theory of positive emotions." This theory proposes that positive emotions broaden our awareness of potential constructive courses of action, allowing us to respond to challenges with more of a "yes" attitude.[205] The theory makes use of the positivity ratio we discussed in Chapter 2. Using that 3 to 1 ratio, we build emotional resilience by creating at least three experiences of positive emotion to counter every single negative emotional experience.[206]

I use this practice of outnumbering my negative emotions with positive ones by keeping a list of things I'm grateful for. We discussed gratitude as a positive emotion in Chapter 2, along with the idea of keeping lists at hand of things for which we are grateful. Gratitude has been linked to not only increased optimism, but also better health, more happiness, improved social connections, and certainly increased emotional resilience.[207] Every time I catch myself angrily ruminating over something, such as the current state of political affairs, I think of three things I'm grateful for, using my list if I have to: i.e., my family, my friends, and how my editor friend Laura always takes my calls! I contemplate each of the three items on the list I've selected and, almost immediately, the unhelpful anger is replaced

---

204. *Learned Optimism*, at 90.

205. *Positivity*, at 21–24 (explaining the broaden and build theory of positive psychology).

206. *Positivity*, at 32; 110.

207. *The Mayo Clinic Handbook for Happiness*, at 92.

by gratitude.[208] I've transformed myself from a ruminating curmudgeon to somebody you might look forward to talking with.

We can also build our emotional resilience through various types of meditation practices which I describe in detail in Chapter 9.

Research shows that the need for emotional resilience involves four major areas of our life: 1) overcoming childhood obstacles, such as abuse or poverty; 2) dealing with everyday stresses such as arguments with friends, problems at work, and financial pressures; 3) working through life-altering events such as death of a loved one, loss of a job, or a divorce; and 4) applying resilience to "reach out so that you can achieve all you are capable of."[209]

The first three areas pertain to how we respond to adversity. The methods we've developed for viewing the world and responding to adversity are not always helpful for establishing wellbeing. For example, when we feel threatened, we may tend to play fast and loose with the truth, take things personally, assume the worst, or just give up.[210] Or, our response to adversity may be to immediately blame the problem on somebody else, particularly if there is a convenient choice from a group against whom we hold a bias. Emotional resilience is the ability to overcome these patterns of response.

The fourth area of emotional resilience is proactive in nature. We seek opportunities to explore and grow our potential, creating for ourselves more opportunities to create greater meaning, connection and richness.[211]

---

208. As I mention elsewhere, sometimes anger is productive, such as when it spurs us to correct social injustice or confront a personal situation in need of effective resolution. *See, e.g.*, Eckman, Dr. Paul. "Anger Can Be Useful." *Psychology Today* https://www.psychologytoday.com/us/blog/face-it/201701/anger-can-be-useful (retrieved April 14, 2019). What I refer to in the text is unhelpful ruminating, brooding, or agonizing over something that prevents us from moving forward in a way that builds wellbeing.

209. *The Resilience Factor*, at 15 (citing work by Ann Masten, Karin Best, and Norman Garmezy: Masten, A., Best, K. & Garmezy, N. (1990). "Resilience and development: Contributions from the study of children who overcome adversity." *Development and Psychopathology*, 2(04):425–444).

210. If any of this rings true for you, I suggest the following book: Ruiz, Don Miquel (1997). *The Four Agreements*. San Rafael, CA: Amber-Allen Publishing.

211. *The Resilience Factor*, at 15; 26–27 (stating that resilience is necessary to sustain a commitment "to the pursuit of learning and new experiences").

Developing this proactive skill is of great value for building wellbeing. As I've mentioned already, we experience great joy when we are able to recognize and develop our full potential and express it in a meaningful way. We satisfy a primary need to affirm ourselves.

Know your cognitive style.

Developing these four areas of emotional resilience requires that we address "our cognitive style." This refers to the way we interpret what we think we hear or see, sometimes looking through the obscuring lens of our self-defeating patterns of thought and behavior.[212] Fortunately, we aren't bound by our childhood trauma or patterns of thought and behavior developed over the years.[213] People can change and grow.

To see clearly, we have to learn to accurately and realistically process information.[214] We need to become scrupulous in evaluating what we see and hear, learning to avoid the obscuring filter of any biased and mistaken beliefs we harbor.[215] Yoga philosophy, which I discuss in some detail in Chapter 10, has long recognized the importance of making sure our thoughts are based in reality and not arising from mistake or our imagination. First, we learn from yoga to pay attention to whether our thoughts are helpful to our wellbeing or harmful. For example, in his *Yoga Sūtras* the sage Patañjali identified thoughts as falling into one of two types: 1) thoughts are either *akliṣṭa*, thoughts arising from a clear mind that help us achieve our goals; or 2) *kliṣṭa*, thoughts that arise from a confused or misdirected mind, leading us away from our goals.[216]

---

212. *The Resilience Factor*, at 11–12.

213. *The Resilience Factor*, at 49–52 (stating that what "is learned can be unlearned," through motivation and application of the right skills).

214. *The Resilience Factor*, at 54–56 (proposing adoption of an attitude of realistic optimism, maintaining "a positive outlook without denying reality, actively appreciating the positive aspects of a situation without ignoring the negative aspects").

215. *The Resilience Factor*, at 54–56.

216. *The Yoga Sūtras of Patañjali*, at 28–29 (discussing Patañjali's *Yoga Sūtra* 1.5).

This is an example of where I use my basic mindfulness test: I ask myself if this thought or emotion is going to help me create more or less wellbeing? If the answer is more, I say "yes" to the thought and see where it goes. However, if the answer is less, I interrupt the thought or emotion and evaluate whether there is a need to pay any further attention to it. While anger, for example, can be a very worthwhile emotion when it causes us to stand up for ourselves or others in response to threat, it can also result in behavior that drives people away from us, limiting wellbeing. So, when I feel anger, I immediately look for its cause and evaluate whether it is serving a useful purpose. Similarly, going back to my car repair example, as soon as I catch myself being self-critical because I don't know much about fixing an auto engine, I stop and ask myself if that thought is even remotely helpful to creating more wellbeing. The answer comes quickly, saving me the negativity of beating myself up emotionally.

Yoga offers us assistance in refining our cognitive style, the way we interpret what is going on around us. Patañjali wrote that thoughts can be placed into five different categories:

- The first category ("right knowledge") consists of thoughts based on accurate, factual information. Here we actually witness something firsthand or learn of something from a highly reliable source. Our thoughts pertaining to what we witnessed are based in fact.[217]

- The second category consists of thoughts based on a mistaken interpretation of an actual fact, an "error," such as mistaking a coiled rope in the road for a cobra. In this case we really did witness something that was real, a rope, but mistakenly believe it to be a snake.[218]

- The third category involves thoughts arising from our "imagination," a conceptualization we make that is not based in any reality; a delusion. An example might be thinking that because somebody didn't call us back or respond to our email within 24

---

217. *The Yoga Sūtras of Patañjali*, at 32–38 (discussing Patañjali's *Yoga Sūtra* 1.7).

218. *The Yoga Sūtras of Patañjali*, at 38–39 (discussing Patañjali's *Yoga Sūtra* 1.8).

hours, they must be angry with us or otherwise not hold us in much regard. In reality, though, the person is in the hospital because he or she is sick or injured and can't even look at their phone or email. We've created a false reality out of our fantasy.[219]

- The fourth category refers to thoughts that arise in a deep sleep.[220]

- The fifth category pertains to our memories, which are based on any of the other four.[221]

These categories underscore the importance of learning how to accurately process information before acting. How often do we get all worked up and even act out based on a mistaken view of the facts or a memory of something we only imagined actually happened? Patañjali's breakdown of the different categories of thought suggests that this occurs more often than we know.

We can develop skills to assist us in better interpreting what we see and hear. These skills can help us make more appropriate choices on our path to building wellbeing. Such skills include paying attention to any false presumptions we might be making when we interpret situations, identifying the belief systems we tend to use, including any bias we carry, learning to be calmer and more focused before speaking or acting in times of stress, and creating methods to stop unhelpful thinking in real time.[222] For assistance in helping yourself develop skills such as these, please consider the resource cited in this footnote.[223]

---

219. *The Yoga Sūtras of Patañjali*, at 39–41 (discussing Patañjali's *Yoga Sūtra* 1.9).

220. *The Yoga Sūtras of Patañjali*, at 41–42 (discussing Patañjali's *Yoga Sūtra* 1.10).

221. *The Yoga Sūtras of Patañjali*, at 43–47 (discussing on Patañjali's *Yoga Sūtra* 1.11; explaining the concept of *saṁskāra*, mental imprints resulting from every experience we have; with memory being the "product of *saṁskāras*"). *See also, The Yoga Sūtras of Patañjali*, at 573 (defining *saṁskāra*).

222. *The Resilience Factor*, at 12–14.

223. *The Resilience Factor*, at 63–321 (providing detailed explanations of each skill, tests to measure current skill levels, and exercises to increase these skills). For this and other reasons, *The Resilience Factor* is a powerful resource for developing emotional resilience, with chapters focused on special advice for developing resilience in relationships, parenting, work, and life in general.

The field of brain science aids in understanding and developing these skills. Using functional magnetic resonance imaging (fMRI) to measure brain activity in response to a variety of circumstances, professionals in this field can tell us quite a bit about how the brain works and responds to various situations.[224] Their ability to "map" the brain helps us understand the roles each part of the brain plays in our patterns of thought and behavior. Using this information, we can learn to recognize and avoid the mental "traps" that get in the way of a life of wellbeing.

One important research finding concerns the subject of neuroplasticity, the brain's ability to grow in such a way as to both reinforce existing connections between parts of the brain, as well as build new ones. Armed with this information, professionals can help us identify and resolve ill-serving patterns of thought through an intentional focus of attention, "a form of self-directed experience," that stimulates new patterns of neural firing and linkages in the brain.[225]

Following are some examples of how work by Dr. Daniel Siegel at the UCLA Medical Center helped patients develop new linkages ("integration") between parts of their brains to help them overcome their unhelpful thought patterns.

1. A rage filled, depressed high school sophomore, diagnosed as possibly being bipolar, was helped by learning mindful awareness, resulting in the gradual expansion of the middle prefrontal areas of his brain and growth of calming fibers.[226]

---

224. Siegel, Dr. Daniel (2011 ed). *Mindsight*. New York, NY: Bantam Books *Mindsight*, at 29. Dr. Siegel, M.D., is an author, psychiatrist, and a clinical professor of psychiatry at the UCLA Medical Center, as well as a founding co-director of UCLA's Mindful Awareness Research Center.

225. *Mindsight*, at 5 (describing neuroplasticity, the brain's "capacity for creating new neural connections and growing new neurons in response to experience"); and at 39-43 (explaining how focus of attention shapes the brain's patterns and architecture). *And see Aware* (Dr. Siegel's therapeutic use of his Wheel of Awareness methodology). These and other of Dr. Siegel's books provide guidance to the reader for implementing this information in his or her own life.

226. *Mindsight*, at 79–101.

2. A 92-year-old attorney, due to a cold, uncaring childhood, had never developed access to the part of his brain responsible for social connection. By stimulating neural growth necessary to re-engage this part of the brain, he learned how to feel love and passion.[227]

3. A married couple in their thirties, after ten years of marriage, were filled with contempt and anger towards each other. Exercises were used to awaken portions of their brains helpful to getting along better, while other parts of the brains that were getting in the way of saving their marriage, were developed so they were able to calm down.[228]

This ability to recognize and understand human patterns of thought and behavior gives each of us hope for learning how to better respond to challenging times. **We can learn to master patterns of thought and emotion that have held us back, the patterns that cause us to create rift instead of connection, reject love and friendship instead of reaching for it, or run from opportunity.** By building our own emotional resilience we attain greater freedom to enrich our lives in ways we can't even yet see.

We now have a blueprint for what a life of wellbeing looks like, those elements we can have in mind to help guide our choices each day. Also, we now have information to help us develop the emotional resilience we need to increase the presence of these elements in our lives. With this information in mind, we turn in Part 2 to a discussion of how yoga is tailor-made for helping us build a life rich in wellbeing.

---

227. *Mindsight*, at 103–119.

228. *Mindsight*, at 210–231.

Part 2

Yoga as a Path to Wellbeing

Chapter 8
Yoga for wellbeing; an overview

The elements of the wellbeing theory are an incredible template for creating a full, rich life. By using these elements, we have a guide for calibrating our thoughts and actions towards becoming the best version of ourselves. However, simply knowing these elements is not enough to maximize well-being in our lives. To fully implement what we now know about wellbeing, we require proficiency in three skills: awareness; the ability to focus; and greater effectiveness in making and sustaining positive connections with ourselves and with others.[229]

Awareness.

We need to be aware in each moment of what is happening around us. Only when we are fully awake to what life is offering us can we recognize and respond effectively to opportunities to build wellbeing. Without awareness, many of these opportunities pass us by unnoticed. When we become skilled at paying attention, we get to choose the direction of our life, rather than letting life choose it for us. In Chapter 2 we discussed the concept of positivity resonance, the way we can connect to others through emotions. For example, we learned that not only can we observe somebody experiencing joy, we can actually share that joy with them if we are paying attention. In Chapter 6 we discussed how mirror neurons play a role in that process. Mirror neurons connect the emotions of two or more people through what are called feedback loops. This process allows us not only to see facial expressions and body language, but also to feel that person's

---

229. *Aware*, at 4–5 (discussing research demonstrating how learning to connect with life with kindness and compassion increases wellbeing).

underlying emotions.[230] If I'm paying sufficient attention to my grandson or granddaughter when they are playing a new song for me on the guitar, I can feel, not just see or hear, their pleasure and pride in how they play. I'm no longer just listening to a song, I'm experiencing it. Such interactions pave the way to deeper connection with our own feelings, as well as closer relationships with others.

To help us cultivate this powerful skill of awareness, we have to learn to calm our minds so that we aren't too "anxious or preoccupied" to catch the cues from another.[231] If we are harried, we miss the warmth of a person's voice, the beginnings of a smile, or perhaps the welling of tears of hurt in the eyes.[232] The more self-absorbed and distracted we are by our own thoughts and emotions, the smaller our world gets, limiting our ability to connect with anyone. Conversely, the more attentive we are to what is going on around us, the better able we will be to accurately and quickly feel another's inner state. Our receptivity creates a greater possibility of wellbeing as "our world expands," not only increasing our ability to relate well with others, but also allowing us to identify interesting activities or worthwhile goals and recognize occasions asking for our meaningful contribution.[233]

We also need to cultivate the skill of self-awareness, what is going on inside us. Self-awareness goes far beyond being attuned to our patterns of thought and emotion. To be the best version of ourselves, we need to discover everything about us. This includes our strengths, those traits we discussed in Chapter 3 that drive us. We need to understand our preferences—what we like to do. And there is even more to us. Self-awareness includes recognizing all the knowledge we've gained through education and life experiences, acknowledging what we are skilled at doing

230. *Social Intelligence*, at 42–43 (describing how mirror neurons work; i.e., pointing out that "the moment someone sees an emotion expressed on your face, they will at once sense that same feeling within themselves").

231. *Social Intelligence*, at 53.

232. *Social Intelligence*, at 53 (offering by example how the author's "defensive reserve" at the start of a trip with strangers initially impeded his ability to connect with them, despite their friendliness towards him, but that, as he relaxed, he was then able to experience the warmth of their personalities).

233. *Social Intelligence*, at 54.

and what we know. For example, my son works in the business world and has an MBA. But he can build a deck, having spent summers working for a building contractor back in high school. We all have things we've learned, knowledge we've accumulated from here and there. And we need to be in touch with our passions, dreams, and desires. Finally, as I discuss in Chapter 10, as a human being, we have the potential to live as the highest expression of what a person can be, which includes being kind, generous, and treating others with dignity. Those attributes are part of what we are capable of being as well. Expressing ourselves fully in the world requires that we fully know each and every aspect of who we are.

As we learned in Part 1, our deepest desire is to uncover our true potential and find a way to manifest it in some meaningful fashion, whether through work, an avocation, or both. This desire for full self-expression is a "central need" of human beings,[234] and has been called the "essence of joy."[235] For this self-expression to occur we must become aware of life around us as well as fully self-aware of all we are, all we have to offer. When we harness all of this "self" and express it in service of something greater than ourselves, we create a high level of wellbeing.[236] Without this deep level of awareness, we will be unable to fully avail ourselves of the joyful, satisfying experience of living a life of full self-expression.[237]

---

234. *The Discovery of Being*, at 80 (quoting Nietzsche to emphasize that we must each discover our unique path in life: "In all the world, there is one specific way that no one but you can take," and if we have the courage to take that path we might know the greatest joy of expressing our most vital essence).

235. *The Discovery of Being*, at 80–83.

236. *Flourish*, at 17 (pointing out that true meaning is not measured subjectively, by how much meaning we attach emotionally to what we've done, but objectively, by how much our actions actually serve something bigger than ourselves).

237. *Man's Search for Meaning*, at 85 (discussing how true meaning requires attention to "what life expects of us." Rather than constantly asking ourselves what the meaning of life might be, we instead learn to "think of ourselves as those who were being questioned by life—daily and hourly" and then responding with the "right action," applying our particular set of assets to do so).

Focus.

The second skill we need to fully implement what we know about wellbeing is the ability to sustain focus on whatever we undertake. The skill of holding our attention is "essential for wellbeing."[238] Having used our skill of awareness to make sound choices that build wellbeing, we want to artfully follow those choices through to completion. This requires the ability to concentrate in the face of disruptions of all types, whether the disruptions are sensory, such as what we see and hear, or emotional, such as a negative thought or emotion that serves no purpose other than to sabotage our efforts at full self-expression.[239]

There are three kinds of focus: inner; other; and outer.[240] "Inner" focus allows us to connect to our inner self, that full potential I described above that includes our strengths, preferences, education, life experiences, knowledge, passions, dreams, desires, and capacity for kindness and the other characteristics of our higher nature. We use this inner focus to weigh choices in terms of compatibility with our dreams and goals, and then as reminders, like the compass of a ship, of what path we've chosen to pursue. The second type of focus, "other" focus, involves how we connect with others. We spoke of this type of focus at length in Chapter 6 in our discussion of deepening positive relationships by sustained, rather than casual, attention to others. And the third type of focus, "outer" focus concerns how we view the world in general.[241] As we discussed in Chapter 4, we use this outer focus to stay attuned to what the world is asking of us in terms of our chance to provide some meaningful service. We use this focus as well by giving thought to the world in general when we consider the effects of what we are about to do or say—we pay attention to the rule of cause and effect. For example, if I spread this rumor, how many people will it end

---

238. *Focus*, at 15 (writing that the "power to disengage our attention from one thing and move it to another is essential for well-being," and that our "selective attention" allows us to stay focused on what we choose to pay attention to, allowing us to become "absorbed" and emotionally experience the full benefits of that absorption); *and see Aware*, at 46–47 (describing a focused attention as a core element for wellbeing).

239. *Focus*, at 14 (discussing the importance of learning to avoid the distractions caused by the senses and our emotions).

240. *Focus*, at 3–4.

241. *Focus*, at 4.

up hurting? Or, if I back off a bit at a partners' meeting about my role in a successful project and praise somebody else, what well-deserved benefits might go his or her way as a result? We need to become proficient at all three of these types of focus in order to effectively stay on track towards increasing wellbeing.[242]

Effective connection.

The third skill we need to maximize wellbeing is the ability to make and sustain positive connections with others.[243] We've discussed the value of connection with others. In fact, as we discussed in Chapter 6, we know from the on-going seventy plus year Harvard Study of Adult Development that our relationships shape our lives, with "the most important contributor to joy and success in adult life" being warm, positive connection with others, according to the study's data.[244]

Yoga is an ideal means for developing these three skills of awareness, focus, and effective connection.

What is yoga?

When some people hear the term "yoga" they immediately picture being asked to perform a pose like Down Dog, a backbend, a twist, or bend over to touch their toes. Their only idea of yoga is that it involves stretching and a variety of postures. That may have been your first thought when you read the title of this chapter: "Oh no, I have to touch my toes to get wellbeing? That isn't going to happen!"

---

242. *Focus*, at 4.

243. *Aware*, at 4–5 (discussing research demonstrating how learning to connect with life with kindness and compassion increases wellbeing).

244. *Triumphs of Experience*, at 52; 369–370.

Yoga is far more than doing yoga poses. **Yoga is a set of practices for furthering a philosophy of living.**[245] Performing poses, called *āsana*, is just one of a number of such practices, which include, among many others, meditation, and breathing techniques, called *prāṇāyama*.[246] I discuss these three more commonly known practices in the next chapter. The particular philosophy of living for which the practices are employed varies depending on the practitioner's yoga tradition or personal life philosophy.[247] Let me explain what I mean by that.

When we study yoga, we are studying over 3,500 years of conversations among people trying to figure out answers to basic life questions, such as: "Who am I?" "Why am I here?" "How can I live safely and in harmony with others and with nature?" And "Is there a God and, if there is, how do I stay on his or her good side?" Over time, many different yoga traditions evolved, each tradition with its own unique answers to such questions. What I refer to as yoga philosophy covers the whole range of these viewpoints.[248]

---

245. *Light on the Yoga Sūtras of Patañjali*, at xvii (stating that "Yoga is an art, a science, and a philosophy"); and 48 (defining "yoga" to be a "means" for "use"); Carrera, Rev. Jaganath (2015, 5th ed); *Inside the Yoga Sūtras*. Buckingham, VA: Integral Yoga Publications, at 10 (defining the word "yoga" to include "practices"). *The Yoga Sūtras of Patañjali*, at 577 (defining "yoga" to mean both a classical school of Indian philosophy as well as a set of various practices).

246. For further discussion of different yoga practices, *see The Yoga Tradition*; *see also* Freeman, Richard and Taylor, Mary (2016). *The Art of Vinyasa*. Boulder, CO: Shambhala Publications, Inc., at 7–35. For further exploration of the range of yoga practices, consider the following resources: White, Dr. David Gordon (2000). *Tantra In Practice*. Princeton, NJ: Princeton University Press; Dyczkowski, Dr. Mark (1987); *The Doctrine of Vibration*. Albany, NY: State University of New York Press; Brooks, Dr. Douglas (1992). *Auspicious Wisdom*. Albany, NY: State University of New York, Albany; Ortega, Dr. Paul-Muller (1989). *The Triadic Heart of Śiva*. Albany, NY: State University of New York Press, Albany; White, Dr. David Gordon (2007 ed.). *The Alchemical Body*. Chicago, IL: The University of Chicago; and Muktibodhananda, Swami (2008 ed). *Haṭha Yoga Pradīpikā*. Mungar, Bihar, INDIA: Bihar School of Yoga.

247. *The Yoga Sūtras of Patañjali*, at 577 (stating "Historically, *Yoga* just referred to a cluster of meditative techniques, some form of which was common to numerous different schools and sects, rather than a distinct philosophical school").

248. There are a number of yoga paths, called *margas*. These include *bhakti-yoga*, a path of devotion to God, *jñāna-yoga*, a path of knowledge and discrimination, *karma-yoga*, a path of duty and action devoted to God, and Patañjali's *dhyāna-yoga*, a path of silent meditation. *The Yoga Sūtras of Patañjali*, at xxiii–xxv. These paths are referenced in, among other places, the very popular *Bhagavad Gita*, believed to have been written somewhere around the fourth century, B.C.E.

Sometimes the viewpoints offered by certain traditions differ in only a nuanced way. Often, however, the differences in viewpoint from one tradition to another can be quite dramatic.[249] For example, on the one hand are dualist traditions, such as the "classical" yoga tradition represented by Patañjali's *Yoga Sūtras*.[250] A tradition is considered "dualist" because it views an Ultimate Reality, by whatever name, as existing separate and distinct from all of creation, including each of us.[251] Because of this separation, Patañjali's dualist yoga teaches a set of "techniques" through which a person seeking a spiritual experience of Ultimate Reality can disentangle himself or herself from the material world, called *prakṛti*, in order to achieve this experience. This spiritual experience can occur only by the practitioner eventually eliminating all connection to the material world, even to his or her thoughts, because even these finite aspects of the material world are separate from Ultimate Reality.[252]

In sharp contrast to dualism are the nondualist traditions. Broadly speaking, nondual traditions view everything in the material world as individual living expressions of Ultimate Reality. These traditions see in

---

249. *The Yoga Tradition*, at 3 (writing that yoga is "a spectacularly multifaceted phenomenon, and as such it is very difficult to define because there are exceptions to every conceivable rule").

250. *The Yoga Sūtras of Patañjali*, at 577 (describing how Patañjali's *Yoga Sūtras* represent the formal classical school of yoga, one of the six formal classical philosophical schools in India). The other Indian classical schools of philosophy are: *Nyāya* (development of rules of logic to govern ongoing debates among the schools); *Vaiśeṣika* (study of metaphysics): *Sāṅkhya* (refers to "enumeration" or categorization, with focus on the twenty-four categories of material reality, the world, called *prakṛti*); *Mīmāṃsā* (focus on determining what is knowledge versus belief, as well as *Vedic* ritual and *dharma*); and *Vedānta* (focus on the interpretation of the *Upaniṣads* related to the relationship between Consciousness, *Brahman* in the *Upaniṣads*, the individual soul, *Atman*, and the material world, *prakṛti*). *The Yoga Sūtras of Patañjali*, at 563–577.

251. *The Yoga Tradition*, at 4 (stating "Patañjali's dualist metaphysics…strictly separates the transcendental Self from Nature (*prakṛti*) and its products"); and at 77 (describing both Patañjali's yoga and the *Sankhya* school as "dualist philosophies," teaching that the "transcendental Selves (*puruṣa*) are radically different from Nature (*prakṛti*)").

252. *The Yoga Sūtras of Patañjali*, at 4–21 (commenting on Patañjali's *Yoga Sūtras* 1.1 and 1.2); *see also The Yoga Sūtras of Patañjali* at 8 (stating that "the soul has to become uncoupled from not just the gross body but the subtle body of the *citta* [thoughts] as well"); and at 9 (commenting that any realization of our divine or transcendental, "innermost conscious self," requires us to fully disengage from all forms of the material world).

the world an "all-embracing unity," rich in diversity but all part of one Ultimate Reality.[253]

In our discussion of yoga philosophy, I share the views of a number of traditions, dualist and nondualist, which I find most conducive to building a life of wellbeing. Of particular application to our discussion of wellbeing is the emergence of nondual tantric traditions somewhere around 100 C.E.[254] The word "*tantra*" means to "extend" or "expand,"[255] and also refers to an "unfolding" or "continuous process" that "extends knowledge" or "expands wisdom."[256] This notion of expanding wisdom refers in part to the fact that the nondual tantric religions sought to preserve certain beliefs, rituals, and practices from dualist traditions while at the same time choosing to embrace life, rather than disentangle themselves from it. These nondualist tantric traditions were troubled by the dualist view that the world was something to be avoided and questioned why they had to remove themselves from worldly entanglements in order to experience Ultimate Reality. They asked questions such as: "Why must we think of the world, and thus the body and mind, as enemies that must be overcome?"

---

253. *The Yoga Tradition*, at 257 (citing excerpts from the *Tejo-Bindu-Upaniṣad*; 6.42).

254. *The Yoga Tradition*, at 341–342 (suggesting that Goddess worship, "central to many Tantric schools, existed already in ancient Vedic times"). Trying to determine dates when talking about yoga history is difficult and dates are often the subject of debate.

255. *The Yoga Tradition*, at 342 (defining "*tantra*" to mean "to extend" or "stretch."); *see, also* Eliade, Mircea (2009 ed.) *Yoga Immortality and Freedom*, Princeton, NJ: Princeton University Press at 200 (defining "*tantra*"to mean "extend."); *and see Tantra The Path of Ecstasy*, Boston, MA: Shambhala Publications, Inc at 1 (defining "*tantra*" to mean "expand").

256. *Yoga Immortality and Freedom*, at 200 (defining "*tantra*" to include the meaning "unfolding" or a continuous process" that "extends knowledge."). *See also Tantra The Path of Ecstasy*, at 1–2 (also defining "*tantra*" to include expanding wisdom). "*Tantra*" also refers to texts that broaden the understanding of yoga "to the point where genuine wisdom arises." *The Yoga Tradition*, at 342. Starting somewhere around 100 C.E., if not earlier, such texts, themselves called *Tantras*, began to appear. There are Buddhist Tantric texts as well as Hindu Tantric texts. *See, generally, The Yoga Tradition*, at Chapter 17, 341–379, for a discussion of some of these texts.

"Why must we limit our experience of being alive in order to follow a spiritual path?[257]

In response to these and other questions, some nondual tantric traditions evolved as a way to reconcile their spiritual views with the wonders and mysteries they found when engaging the world in their daily lives. For example, they certainly wanted to partake of positive emotions—the joy of a delightful surprise gathering of friends, gratitude towards their neighbors who helped them in challenging times, serenity in those times when the work was done, there was plenty of food and shelter, and all was safe, interest in meeting somebody from a strange land, visiting a new place, or hearing a fresh idea, hope for a good crop, the pride of providing for each other during a cold winter while sharing a meal in front of a roaring fire, amusement from watching their kids play, inspiration from observing somebody demonstrate competency in a difficult skill, awe that comes from seeing a rainbow, admiring a soaring eagle, or marveling at the tremendous power of a dark, thundering storm, and, perhaps most important of all, love that comes from the shared experience of connecting with others. These early nondual tantric practitioners also no doubt felt the personal satisfaction that came from contributing their strengths in meaningful service to their friends and neighbors. They knew what it meant to get lost in engaging activities and accomplishing goals, big and small.

These nondual tantric traditions saw the presence of Ultimate Reality in all of life and chose to embrace life as a result, striving for what we've called wellbeing. As a result, these traditions developed by expanding the "wisdom" of dualist traditions in a way that allowed them to fully experience life while still following the spiritual path of their choice. Rather than seeking to "liberate," themselves from the material world, these traditions

---

257. *The Yoga Tradition*, at 341–343 (recognizing that these ideas of fully experiencing life while honoring a spiritual path can be traced back at least as far as the *Upaniṣads*, predating the beginning of the Common Era). While there are a number of different tantric traditions, for our purposes we need not delve into the distinctions of each tradition, and I will simply use the term "nondual tantra or tantric." For an excellent overview of many of these traditions, consider Dr. Feuerstein's *The Yoga Tradition*, particularly Chapter 17, "The Esotericism of Medieval Tantra-Yoga," at 341–379. Also consider his book *Tantra The Path of Ecstasy*, and a course offered by Dr. Douglas Brooks: CC202 *Tantrism: History, Teachings, and Practices*, available at his website: https://rajanaka.com/course-list; retrieved November 16, 2018.

instead sought a passionate engagement with life, living with curiosity and looking for an experience of connection with the divine Ultimate Reality within themselves and in the world.

To facilitate this passionate engagement with life while following their spiritual path, certain of these traditions employed a metaphysical cosmology describing the nature of Ultimate Reality and how that Reality chose to create and continues to create the world. They even ascribed certain personal attributes to that Reality, including, for example, the desire for full expression, benevolence, and dignity. They did this so that they could better recognize Ultimate Reality within themselves and also in others. I discuss these attributes in Chapter 10 as part of my discussion of how the study of yoga philosophy can guide us to our own highest nature, how profoundly wonderful and gracious we as human beings are capable of being in the world when we choose to live as the best version of ourselves and look for it in others and all around us.[258]

In summary, then, **yoga is both a methodology and a philosophy** we can apply to continually calibrate our life towards increased wellbeing.[259]

---

258. The mythological cosmology to which I refer is known as the *Tattvas* ("that-ness," "element," or "category of truth"), a subject beyond the scope of this book. Much of what I've learned about the *Tattvas* come from oral teachings, primarily from Dr. Douglas Brooks, Professor of Religion at the University of Rochester, John Friend, the founder of Anusara Yoga, and several former and current Anusara teachers, including Amy Ippoliti, Jamie Allision, and Madhuri Martin. If you have an interest in learning more about them, consider a course offered by Dr. Douglas Brooks: CC402 *Tattva Theory*, available at his website, https://rajanaka.com/course-list; retrieved November 10, 2018, and an online short course by Dr. Brooks: "YogaSūtra: The Principles of Organized Reality, Teachings on Tattva Theory," available at the Glo website, https://www.yogaglo.com/preview/class/3385; retrieved November 10, 2018. *See also* Shantanada, Swami (2003). *The Splendor of Recognition*. South Fallsburg, NY: Siddha Yoga Publications.

259. Dr. Douglas Brooks has suggested that "yoga" is a "salubrious adjustment" we learn to make in each moment in order to maximize our experience of life. Elaborating, fellow yoga teacher Randall Buskirk pointed out that the word "salubrious" refers to health, prosperity, and wellbeing, while the word "adjustment" is based on words that include the root word for yoga, "*yuj*," meaning "to move towards" or "calibrate." Yoga is, therefore, an ongoing calibration we perform as we make choices that can move us towards a more healthy, prosperous life, a life of wellbeing. See the YouTube video "What is yoga?" by Randall Buskirk: https://www.youtube.com/watch?v=lQQvK12v5SE&feature=youtu.be, retrieved October 15, 2018.

We use yoga to make our life "purposeful, useful, and noble."[260]

How does yoga work?

How does yoga help us achieve the three skills of awareness, focus, and more effective connection with ourselves and with others? The secret of yoga's success lies in both its practices and philosophy. By engaging in yoga's practices properly and regularly, we are able to create and maintain a clear mind. With a clear mind we cease being a victim of the never-ending distracting chatter of thoughts and emotions that can cloud our sense of what is going on around us and within us. The outside world no longer draws our attention away through our senses except when we choose to allow the senses to explore. Out of this greater mental clarity we are far more likely to recognize opportunities for wellbeing and make choices that better serve us. Then, with an increased ability to focus, we are better able to see those choices through to successful fruition.[261] We open the door to a greater understanding of ourselves, better recognizing our full potential so that we can experience the joy and satisfaction of living life fully as an expression of that potential.

Let me give an example from my own pre-yoga life of how a lack of mental clarity can inhibit our ability to avail ourselves of opportunities for greater wellbeing.[262] A number of years ago I was working late but knew I needed to leave the office and hustle if I wanted to get to the gym for a workout before it closed. In addition to enjoying the workout, I had an additional motivation for wanting to work out: one of the main reasons

---

260. *Light on the Yoga Sūtras of Patañjali*, at xvii. *See also The Yoga Tradition*, at 3 (commenting that, despite different viewpoints on what constitutes yoga among the many branches and schools of Yoga, each agree that yoga involves a "state of being or consciousness, that is truly extraordinary." The author concluded that yoga "is a technology of ecstasy, or self-transcendence. How this ecstatic condition is interpreted and what means are employed for its realization differ...from school to school").

261. *The Yoga Sūtras of Patañjali*, at 47–60 (commenting on Patañjali's *Yoga Sūtras* 1.12 to 1.16).

262. This story is from Chapter 76 of *Finding the Midline*, at 232–234.

I pumped iron was so that I would look good in order to attract a date. I know, pretty shallow, but there you go.

I got in the elevator and a few floors down the doors opened and a really nice, pleasant woman entered the elevator. She smiled, said hello, and announced she was heading to the bar/restaurant downstairs because she needed a drink after a tough day at work. I immediately started thinking about how nice it would be to join her. But then my chattering mind kicked in, telling me on the one hand she would never be interested in me, and on the other hand, it didn't matter because I had to get to the gym. Can't miss a workout!

My elevator companion talked to me the entire ride down to the main floor, but I wasn't really listening, although I'm sure I made some outward attempt to nod, smile, and appear to pay attention. Instead, while worrying about whether I'd make it to the gym in time, my brain was also trying to think of witty things to say to attract her interest. Of course, as I already mentioned, yet another part of my brain was telling me not to even bother; why would she want a drink with the "likes of me?" Even though there were only two of us in the elevator, there were quite a few conversations going on. Unfortunately, they were mostly all in my prattling mind.

The elevator reached the main floor and the doors started to open. She turned to me and said: "Well, I guess I'll have to have that drink by myself," and, with that she exited the elevator to head towards the bar. I guess that while I had been conversing with myself, she must have said something about our having a drink together. How would I know? I had too many other voices to listen to. Anyway, the elevator doors closed, and a few minutes later I was several miles down the freeway driving to the gym for that all-important workout.

Suddenly, at about the 50th Street overpass on Rt. 35W in Minneapolis, it hit me: "Wait a minute. Why are you going to the gym when you could be having a drink with her? The only reason you're so obsessed with getting in your workout is so that someday you might be able to attract a woman like her. What are you doing?" I wish I could say I turned around, went back to the bar and had the drink, living happily ever after with her. But, no. Instead, I kept on driving to the gym and did my workout. Over the next several weeks I tried to figure out who she was. But you guessed it: I never saw her again. It was a lost opportunity.

I share this story to illustrate the value of learning how to pay attention by stilling the chattering of our mind, an essential skill for creating the awareness we need to build wellbeing. Yoga is a methodology for controlling these ongoing fluctuations of the mind, the constant flow of thoughts that can blind us to opportunity and even result in our saying and doing things we later regret. Yoga teaches us how to master that distracting chatter, including emotions that tend to arise, so we can connect with ourselves in the moment and properly process the experience of each moment in present time. **Yoga practices instill in us the ability to create a pause or space, mentally and emotionally, so we can properly and fully evaluate what is happening right then.** In fact, yoga has often been defined as "the stilling of the changing states of the mind."[263]

When we learn through yoga to control the constant stream of competing thoughts and feelings in our mind, we are then able to see clearly the best choices for ourselves. In yoga, this state of mind is called a *sattvic* state of mind, meaning that the mind becomes lucid, tranquil, discriminating, and able to make the wisest decisions in the moment, unhampered by bias, prejudice, or emotional flareups.[264] Through the practice of yoga the mind becomes a "harmonized, luminous state of intelligence that allows us to see things as they really are."[265]

---

263. *The Yoga Sūtras of Patañjali*, at 10.

264. *The Yoga Sūtras of Patañjali*, at 573 (describing the three *guṇas*, qualities of being. In addition to *sattva*, the *guṇa* of *tamas* is a state of mind dominated by ignorance, delusion, or by disinterest or a "disinclination toward constructive activity" [at 574], and the *guṇa* of *rajas* is a state of mind dominated by restlessness, passion, or creative activity [at 572); *but see Finding the Midline*, at 137–139 (discussing the *guṇas* and noting that there are times when we benefit from increased *tamas*, such as when we need to cool our passionate fire, calm our mind, or slow down precipitous action, or when we benefit from *rajas* when we need to be more energetic in some situations).

265. *The Art of Vinyasa*, at 39.

Developing a lucid, discriminating mind is a foundational skill and purpose of yoga.[266] Through yoga we learn to control our mind's reactions to our everyday experiences, enabling us to "enjoy and find meaning" in the moments of our life.[267] **We learn through yoga to assert "mastery over consciousness," the way our mind "filters and interprets everyday experiences."[268] We learn to be in charge of ourselves.**[269] In this way we can achieve with greater frequency an "optimal state of inner experience" by bringing "order" to our thoughts.[270] Even more so than the monastic mental and physical routines and spiritual exercises of a thousand years ago used to control attention, the discipline of yoga is ideally suited for this purpose.[271]

Had I been a yoga practitioner during my elevator encounter, the odds are much greater that I would have paid undivided attention to my guest in the elevator and quickly eliminated any notion of a trip to the gym. Listening to her, instead of paying attention to my competing mental conversations, I would have realized that it was far more important to skip the barbells that night and, instead, pursue this potentially exciting new relationship. However, back then I hadn't learned to relax my mind and be aware in the moment, necessary skills for becoming more effective in creating relationship.

---

266. *The Yoga Sūtras of Patañjali*, at 10–21 (commenting on Patañjali's Yoga Sūtra 1.2).

267. *Flow*, at 19.

268. *Flow*, at 9.

269. *Flow*, at 103–106 (discussing yoga and martial arts as examples of engagement). For a martial artist's perspective, I suggest a book written by my friend and professional Jiu Jitsu competitor Mark Genco: Genco, Mark (2017). *Inner Jiu Jitsu*. Denver, CO: Mark Genco. In addition to practicing Jiu Jitsu, Mark is a brilliant yoga teacher and practitioner and has a master's degree in Buddhist Studies. He is also one of the funniest people I know.

270. *Flow*, at 6 (Emphasis in original).

271. *Flow*, at 104 (referring to monastic practices by Saint Benedict and Saint Dominick, as well as the spiritual exercises of Saint Ignatius of Loyola).

Chapter 9
Yoga practices

Yoga practices develop awareness, including self-awareness, increase our ability to focus, and deepen our ability to more effectively connect with others. Three of the most well-known practices are meditation, *āsana* (yoga poses), and *prāṇāyāma* (breathing practices).[272] In this chapter we'll discuss each of these three practices.

Meditation.

A regular meditation practice is essential for maximizing wellbeing. Meditation teaches us mental clarity, how to pay attention to our surroundings and to ourselves, unhampered by distraction. This mental clarity shapes the content and quality of our lives, determining "how we experience and navigate the world."[273]

---

272. *The Art of Vinyasa*, at 7–32 (discussion of the internal forms of yoga practice, including: breath work; *mantra* (sound repetition, for example); *dṛṣṭi* (focused external and internal gaze); *bandhas* (focused points of internal body actions); and *mudrās* (ritualized gestures or internal patterns formed in response to *bandhas*).

273. Salzberg, Sharon (2011). *Real Happiness, The Power of Meditation*. New York, NY: The Workman Publishing Company, Inc., at 8–9. I recommend this book for a very helpful introduction to meditation and how it works. Ms. Salzberg is a best-selling author and a co-founder of the Insight Meditation Society, a center for learning and deepening meditation practice, located in Barre, Massachusetts. She is an internationally recognized meditation teacher, particularly of Buddhist practices such as *Vipassana* (insight) meditation, and *Metta* (loving-kindness) meditation.

We learn through meditation to concentrate without interruption on whatever we've decided is important.[274] With mental clarity, unimpeded by mental chatter and external sensory distractions, we are able to make better choices, promoting our wellbeing in each moment, rather than diminishing it. For example, when we pay undivided attention to a friend or family member during a conversation, rather than split our attention between them and our phone, the television, or whatever else we are thinking about, we are far more likely to notice their excitement or that something is bothering them. We'll notice these things by the tone of their voice, body language, choice of words, or facial expression. By paying attention to them, we are able to meaningfully respond to them in a way that builds that relationship rather than creates a crack in it. Intimate positive relationships are built this way, by paying attention to each other. People are more likely to drift out of relationships when they feel they aren't being heard or seen.

Through a regular meditation practice, we not only become a master of our mind, we also become a master over our words and actions. This happens because, over time and with practice, meditation teaches us to literally watch ourselves thinking. We develop what feels like a space or pause between the thought itself, and our mental reaction to it. We learn to observe the thought in this space, this pause. This allows us to examine those thoughts and emotions before speaking or acting. As a result, we make "better, more informed" and "creative" decisions and actions.[275] We become more centered, better able to deal with the uncertainty and stresses of daily life. No longer prisoner to unhelpful patterns of thought and emotion, we become more refined in our ability to recognize and respond with integrity and grace to life's opportunities as they present themselves. We speak and act in ways that serve our best interests, critical for developing emotional resilience and for more fully recognizing and embracing life's invitations to wellbeing.[276]

---

274. Goleman, Dr. Daniel and Davidson, Dr. Richard J. (2017). *Altered Traits*. New York, NY: Penguin Random House LLC., at 38 (describing how insight meditation increases understanding of our thoughts and emotions); and at 132 (reporting on research results demonstrating that "meditation leads to better sustained attention").

275. *Real Happiness*, at 11.

276. *Real Happiness*, at 12 (discussing how developing our skill of awareness allows us to "connect fully and directly with whatever life brings").

How do we know that meditation does all these things? There is ongoing research on the effectiveness of meditation, looking into questions such as what meditation techniques work, how do they work, and do the benefits last? For example, I mentioned fMRIs in Chapter 7. Using brain imaging, fMRI, neuroscientists have demonstrated how, through various meditation practices, brain cells learn to coordinate in patterns to build parts of the brain responsible for decision-making, memory, "emotional flexibility," and how we respond to stress.[277] Researchers use other methods as well, with each shedding light on the values of meditation.

There are many different types of meditation, and I will reference only some of them here.[278] Each, in its own way, offers us the opportunity to increase our ability to build wellbeing. In addition, research demonstrates that there are also physical, psychological, and emotional benefits from meditation that significantly improve our quality of life. For example, studies suggest that meditation and other mind-body awareness practices, such as yoga, *Qigong*, and *Tai Chi*, can promote healthy cellular growth to encourage healthy aging.[279]

Attention-based meditation practices.

Certain meditation practices are considered to be "attention-based." These practices involve directing and sustaining our attention on some sort of anchor like the breath or our thoughts. Research demonstrates that watching the breath as a type of meditation practice is particularly helpful for increasing mental calmness.[280] A recognized value of watching and noting our thoughts or emotions, called *vipassana*, or insight meditation, is that it enhances our ability for selective attention, the ability to sustain our focus.[281]

---

277. *Real Happiness*, at 25–32.

278. For a discussion of different types of meditation, *see* Fontana, Dr. David (2002 ed). *The Meditator's Handbook*. London, ENG: Thorsons.

279. *The Telomere Effect*, at 100–121; 153–158 (discussing the role of stress reduction for health and suggesting a variety of practices to deal with stress).

280. *Altered Traits*, at 67–68 (citing research from Germany).

281. *Altered Traits*, at 144–145 (discussing study results of *Vipassana* practitioners).

Yet another form of attention-based practice is called Meta-awareness in which we practice watching ourselves think. We pay attention to our attention itself, "noticing, for example, when our mind has wandered off from something we want to focus on."[282] This type of practice helps us to not only recognize unhelpful thought patterns but, by learning to do so, gradually rob them of their power over us. By monitoring ourselves we become master of our mind, spotting an unhelpful thought or emotion, such as a bias, self-doubt, or anger, in the moment but not be swept away by it. We develop the ability to notice such thoughts or emotions as we continue to pay attention to whatever else is going on around us.[283]

The ability to monitor thoughts and emotions in present time is a particularly invaluable aid to building emotional resilience. By immediately noticing and halting, in the heat of the moment, self-defeating patterns of thought or emotions, we prevent them from sabotaging our efforts at creating wellbeing. For example, can you think of a time when you became angry with a friend, workmate, partner, or relative and said something you later wish you hadn't? We can apologize all we want, and try to explain our comments, but words matter; they can inflict lasting damage to the recipient and to the relationship. Wouldn't it be better, in many cases, not to say such things in the first place?

Some attention-based meditation practices focus on an object, or *mantra*, a word or phrase recited out loud or internally. Focusing on an object is a yoga practice taught by Patañjali in his *Yoga Sūtras* to which I've referred earlier.[284] I'll return to Patañjali's method of meditation later in this section. Another type of attention-based meditation practice is the practice taught as part of the Mindfulness-Based-Stress-Reduction ("MBSR") program created by Jon Kabat-Zin at the University of Massachusetts Medical School. MBSR teaches mindfulness to help people with issues such as severe pain. The practice includes focus on the breath, a body

---

282. *Altered Traits*, at 141.

283. *Altered Traits*, at 141–142 (describing how a Meta-awareness practice helps us learn to monitor our mind).

284. *The Yoga Sūtras of Patañjali*, at 4–21 (commenting on Patañjali's *Yoga Sūtras* 1.1 and 1.2). Patañjali also described the practice of reciting and contemplating the sacred syllable *Om*, representing the name for *Īśvara*, the "teacher of the ancients." *See The Yoga Sūtras of Patañjali*, at 103-116 (commenting on Patañjali's *Yoga Sūtras* 1.26–1.28).

scan, and other components. This particular form of meditation practice has been the subject of over six hundred published studies.[285] Among its benefits, research demonstrated MBSR is highly effective in pain reduction and management in the elderly.[286] Other benefits shown through research include an increased ability to focus (orienting, the ability to direct attention),[287] and reduced feelings of loneliness.[288]

Yet another attention-based meditation practice is Kirtan Kriya. This form of meditation involves coordinating the chanting of specific sounds with finger movements in a certain specified repeated pattern. Research demonstrated that this form of meditation improves brain functioning, including increased memory, improved energy, and sharpened attention, among other benefits.[289]

---

285. *Altered Traits*, at 166.

286. *Altered Traits*, at 167 (*citing* Morone, Natalie, et al (2016). "A Mind-Body Program for Older Adults with Chronic Low Back Pain: A Randomized Trial." *JAMA Internal Medicine* 176:3, at 329–37.

287. *Altered Traits*, at 129–130; 144–45 (*citing* Jha, Amishi, et al (2007). "Mindfulness Training Modifies Subsystems of Attention." *Cognitive, Affective, & Behavioral Neuroscience* 7:2, at 109-19; http://www.ncbi.nlm.nih.gov/pubmed/17672382

288. *Altered Traits*, at 176 (*citing* Creswell, J.D., et al (2012). "Mindfulness-Based-Stress Reduction Training Reduction Training Reduces Loneliness and Pro-Inflammatory Gene Expression in Older Adults: A Small Randomized Controlled Trial." *Brain, Behavior, and Immunity*. 26, at 1095–1101.

289. Reynolds, Susan. "Yoga and Kirtan Kriya Meditation Bolster Brain Functioning." *Psychology Today* June 1, 2016; https://www.psychologytoday.com/us/blog/prime-your-gray-cells/201606/yoga-and-kirtan-kriya-meditation-bolster-brain-functioning, retrieved September 27, 2018 (discussing this practice). Research also demonstrated that practicing this particular form of meditation for twelve minutes over a two-month period significantly increased the production of an enzyme, telomerase, important for healthy cell renewal and increased immunity; *The Telomere Effect*, at 59–64; 155–156 (discussing this type of meditation practice).

Loving kindness meditation practice.

In addition to attention-based meditation practices, other types of meditation offer great benefit, with each type influencing the brain in different ways.[290] Some practices seek to develop a particular feeling or attitude, such as compassion or loving kindness.[291] In a loving kindness meditation practice, the meditator wishes themselves well, then, in a progression, wishes others well, including those who have caused them harm or whom they find it difficult to be around.[292] This type of practice builds compassion, altruism, and boosts "the brain's circuits for joy and happiness."[293] It increases neural connections in the brain from which compassion originates and is very effective for increasing feelings of kindness.[294]

One of the most profound changes I've noticed in myself over time is an increased sense of self-acceptance from this practice. In a recording of a loving kindness practice guided by teacher Sharon Salzberg she asks us to offer loving kindness to somebody with whom we are having friction. She then softly follows up by saying: "And, if that is not possible for you today, then offer loving kindness to yourself, because, today, you are the one who needs some kindness." (I am paraphrasing). When this happens, I follow her instructions and repeat her suggested *mantra* to myself: "May I be safe, be happy, be healthy, and live with ease." I find myself relaxing as I let go of whatever undercurrent of anxiety within me that I've associated with the other person. In my experience, what is releasing is the negative attitudes I've been directing towards myself as blame for the friction. Free of those attitudes, I find myself treating myself, and then others, with more kindness.

---

290. *Altered Traits*, at 67-69 (discussing how meditation "is not a single activity but a wide range of practices, all acting in their own particular ways in the mind and brain").

291. *The Mayo Clinic Handbook for Happiness*, at 202.

292. *Altered Traits*, at 104 (describing a loving kindness practice).

293. *Altered Traits*, at 68; 101–112 (reporting that loving kindness meditation "boosts the connections between the brain's circuits for joy and happiness and the prefrontal cortex, a zone critical for guiding behavior," leading to greater altruism the more a person practices this type of meditation).

294. *Altered Traits*, at 115 (reporting that loving kindness meditation increases warm thoughts and feelings about others, literally increasing our feelings of kindness).

Thought-based and contemplative meditation practices.

Another type of meditation practice is thought-based meditation. In this type of practice, the meditator contemplates a particular thought, watching what arises in the mind out of that contemplation. Through this process the meditator may be able to trace the thought to its origin—"what prejudices, biases, assumptions, fears, or other underlying beliefs cause me to think this way?" Then, through reflection, the meditator can do the work necessary to unwind those foundational beliefs that are unhelpful.[295] As an example, we might behave in a way we consider selfish, and then immediately label ourselves as a selfish person. If we meditate on that thought, examining where it comes from, we might remember that we have done all sorts of generous things and aren't selfish at all. We might remember, upon reflection, that we developed a habit of holding on to our money over the years when we didn't have much but are now in a better financial position; i.e., we can afford to be a bit more generous. We're not selfish at all. Or, we realize that we are selfish and hopefully reflecting on that fact might cause change.

A related type of meditation is contemplative meditation, a practice in which a person focuses on a particular word or phrase and, through that focus, develops greater insight into the significance of the word or phrase. For example, by contemplating the word "our" in "The Lord's Prayer" ("Our Father who art in Heaven...") we initially might realize that our concept of "our" doesn't include certain races, religions, cultures, the opposite gender, or some other distinction. This might happen, for example, if the first pictures that arise in our mind as we contemplate the word are only visions of people of our same race, culture, and gender. If we choose, we can then begin to contemplate who else might be included under the meaning of the word "our." We note if we feel any resistance when a vision of a person of a different race, culture, or gender arises in our attempt to contemplate a more inclusive definition of "our." Continuing to contemplate in an attempt to be more inclusive in our attitude, perhaps we stir our memories to recall somebody of that group whom we know to be funny, kind, or who has helped us out. This might result in expanding our definition of the concept of "our" to include somebody from that group. Over

---

295. *The Mayo Clinic Handbook for Happiness*, at 202 (describing the practice of choosing a thought and then focusing on it to the exclusion of all other thoughts. The goal is to experience insight into ourselves and our relationship with the world).

time, as we continue to practice this type of contemplative meditation, we may even begin to expand our definition of "our" to include all humans and, possibly, all living things.[296] Imagine how that attitude would open the door to a more interesting life, rich with stimulating relationship.

Making meditation benefits permanent.

There is evidence suggesting that changes to the brain from meditation can eventually become permanent. Researchers have identified "altered traits," neurologically measurable behavioral changes that arise from a serious meditation practice and last beyond the immediate "afterglow" of the meditation.[297] By "afterglow" I mean that we can remain a kinder person for more than five minutes after we complete a loving-kindness meditation. Examples of altered traits include compassion, improvements in attention for beginners, improved reaction to stress, and reduction in harmful inflammation.[298]

How much meditation does it take to affect an altered trait, a lasting change in behavior such as increased calm, greater awareness, or becoming a kinder and more compassionate person? While more research needs to be done, it appears that to maximize the effects of meditation and perhaps achieve an altered trait, we need a daily practice conducted over years, supplemented with retreats, including "intense booster sessions," and repeated exposure to a well-trained teacher or coach.[299] However, even short-term improvements can be maintained with ongoing, proper practice. So, the sooner we begin a practice, the sooner we will have results and those results will be ongoing so long as we practice.

---

296. As an introduction to this form of contemplative practice, *see* Keating, Thomas (2009 ed.). *Intimacy with God: An Introduction to Centering Prayer.* New York, NY: The Crossroads Publishing Company. *See also* Frenette, David (2017 ed). *The Path of Centering Prayer.* Boulder, CO: Sounds True; *and see* Merton, Thomas (1996 ed). *Contemplative Prayer.* New York, NY: Image.

297. *Altered Traits*, at 6–7.

298. *Altered Traits*, at 273.

299. *Altered Traits*, at 144; 258–259.

Patañjali's meditation practice.

Meditation is the central practice of Patañjali's yoga, and a practice adopted by many yoga traditions. The ultimate objective of Patañjali's yoga is "realization" of the "innermost conscious self," our soul, through the meditative practices contained in his *Yoga Sūtras*.[300] This realization occurs through a process of learning how to quiet the mind and developing a single-pointed focus, typically on an object.[301] Through maintaining this focus the meditator's attention moves ever deeper inward, away from sensory distractions of the outside world. The inner world of thoughts and emotions become quieted, allowing the practitioner to become totally absorbed in the object of the meditation.

Patañjali's meditation methodology is laid out in such detail that his *Yoga Sūtras* have been called "a manual for the practitioner."[302] In the second chapter of Patañjali's *Yoga Sūtras*, *Sādhana Pāda* ("Chapter on Practice"), he describes what collectively is called the "eight limbs of yoga."[303] **Each of the eight limbs contributes in its own way to helping us develop the three skills I've discussed, awareness, focus, and the ability to more effectively connect with ourselves and with others. Therefore, we must understand and practice each in order to gain the full benefit of Patañjali's meditation methodology.**

The eight limbs, presented in the order Patañjali discussed them, are:

1. *Yama* (rules for how to behave in society: non-harming; truthfulness; non-stealing; sexual propriety; and lack of greed);

---

300. *The Yoga Sūtras of Patañjali*, at xvii (stating that Patañjali's teachings focused on realization of the *puruṣa*, the term used by the Indian philosophical school of Yoga to refer to the "innermost conscious self, loosely equivalent to the soul in Western Greco-Abrahamic traditions").

301. *The Yoga Sūtras of Patañjali*, at liii–lviii (providing an overview of the goals of Patañjali's yoga).

302. *The Yoga Sūtras of Patañjali*, at lvii.

303. The methodology I describe in the text does not include discussion of the deepening levels of inner realization described in the first chapter of Patañjali's *Yoga Sūtras*, titled *Samādhi Pāda*, the chapter (*Pāda*) on "Meditative Absorption" (*Samādhi*).

2. *Niyama* (rules for how to take care of ourselves: cleanliness, purification of ourselves, both inside and out; contentment; burning desire to transform; study of sacred scriptures and self-study; and devotion to God).[304]

3. *Prāṇāyāma* (breath work);

4. *Āsana* (poses or postures);

5. *Pratyāhāra* (withdrawal of the senses inward);

6. *Dhāranā* (single-pointed concentration);

7. *Dhyāna* (sustained concentration; meditation); and

8. *Samādhi* (meditative absorption; realization of the soul).

These eight limbs are the "means" Patañjali provides for helping us build a "discriminative discernment," a mind free of distractions. They teach us the ability to sustain a single-pointed focus so we can better attain our goals, whether it is realization of our soul, greater connection to something bigger than us, such as our community, or both. These limbs guide us to a deeper understanding of ourselves while at the same time optimizing our ability to connect effectively with others as well as with ourselves. Whether we seek deeper spiritual connection, greater wellbeing in our life, or both, these eight limbs provide the roadmap for us, helping us develop the mastery of our consciousness necessary to enrich our lives.[305]

How do the eight limbs help us develop this mastery of consciousness? The first two, the *yamas* and *niyamas*, are an ethical system that helps us

---

304. Viewing Patañjali's *Yoga Sūtras* as a methodology for realization of the soul, *puruṣa*, it is important to note that the fifth of five *niyamas* is *Īśvara Pranidhāna* (surrender to God—*Īśvara*; *Yoga Sūtra* 2.45). Patañjali wrote that surrender and devotion, *Bhakti*, to God, can itself lead to "the ultimate goal of yoga—the cessation of all thought, *sampra-jñāta-samādhi*, and realization of the *puruṣa* [soul]. *The Yoga Sūtras of Patañjali*, at 82–83 (commenting on *Yoga Sūtra* 1.23).

305. *Flow*, at 103–106 (describing how both Patañjali's eight limbs and martial arts are means for gaining ultimate control of the mind).

direct our energy and minimize disruption in our life due to bad choices we might otherwise make. The *yamas* and *niyamas* help us "reduce psychic entropy" by changing our attitudes in how we treat others and ourselves.[306] By lessening the distractions that often arise from mistreatment of others or ourselves, we are better able to channel our attention.[307] **To maximize wellbeing in our life, we must learn how to treat others and ourselves in a way that invites rather than deters connection,** that fosters rather than stifles self-respect and our own dignity.

Practicing rules for treating others, the *yamas*, are necessary if we seek more harmonious interaction with people. When we treat people well, we aren't distracted by having to constantly look over our shoulder because we gossiped about somebody and caused them harm, lied to a friend or family member, stole something, sexually harassed a person or took advantage of them, or are overwhelmed with envy for what other people possess or ruled by greed over keeping what we think is ours. Removing or lessening these behaviors and attitudes is a giant step towards creating mental clarity because we rid ourselves of distractions attributable to such behaviors. This clarity allows us to better focus on more important matters such as recognizing when our friends are excited, or our customer is unhappy. Our mind is free to be more receptive to positive thoughts such as gratitude or savoring something well done. We are better able to remember and explore all aspects of what makes us who we are, ranging from our strengths to our dreams and visions.

We take another big step towards creating wellbeing in our lives when we practice the *niyamas*. We take care of ourselves, keep fit, watch our diet, and avoid or limit stimulants that eventually tire us out. We study what makes us tick through therapy and increased self-awareness, read uplifting,

---

306. *Flow*, at 104.

307. *Flow*, at 104 (discussing how following the rules of the *yamas* and *niyamas* help clear the way for us to channel our attention "into predictable patterns," making attention easier to control); *and see The Yoga Sūtras of Patañjali*, at 252 (discussing the proposition that following the *yamas* can be categorized as a moral system because they encourage "moral means of interacting with others"). *But see Hatha Yoga Pradīpikā*, at 4–7 (discussing problems that can arise from rigidly imposing rules of conduct on one's self without having first created a balanced body, mind, and energy through hatha yoga practices).

inspiring books, and care about others.[308] Connecting to our inner self is much easier when our stomach isn't growling, our low back isn't sore, or our inner demons aren't running roughshod through our brain, taking over our otherwise "quiet, reflective" time. Further, research studying the behavior of telomeres, the very ends of our chromosomes, lend credibility to Patañjali's rules of self-care. Research in this area shows that attention to proper diet, exercise, and stress factors in our lives helps us remain more resilient as we age, even in the face of diseases such as cancer.[309]

The third and fourth limbs of *āsana* and *prāṇāyāma*, poses and breathing exercises, are practices that help us to control our body and senses so we can better concentrate.[310] I discuss these two limbs in separate sections below. While some meditation practices, like breath-focused practices, use the senses as an anchor or object of focus, the senses can also serve as tremendous distractions at times. This is particularly the case when we are trying to connect with another person, but our mind is pulled away by the buzzing of our phone, an interesting person walking by, something on the television, a noise, or any number of other things that attract our senses and, thus, our attention, away from that person. *Āsana* and *prāṇāyāma*, when practiced for this purpose, are highly effective for teaching us how to be in charge of our attention even as the senses seek to distract us. We learn to move our attention away from such distraction as we direct it towards total absorption in the object of our focus—whether parts of the body in a pose or our breath in breathing exercises. This is also excellent

---

308. The practice of the fourth *niyama*, *svādhyāya*, study of sacred, uplifting scriptures and self-study, *Yoga Sūtra* 2.44, provides a vehicle for self-realization. By diligent, devoted practice, the inspiring knowledge imparted from the scriptures penetrate our being. Over time we become so infused with uplifting energy that in times of challenge our mind will naturally turn to the uplifting, the sacred, so influencing our thoughts and actions that we become transformed into living embodiments of those scriptures. Chidvilasananda, Swami (1997). *Enthusiasm*. South Fallsburg, NY: SYDA Foundation, at 43–46. *And see Enthusiasm*, at 57–58 (describing how recitation of sacred *mantra* infuses us with the dignity of the sacred chants). In that regard, *see The Yoga Sūtras of Patañjali*, at 109–116 (commenting on Patañjali's *Yoga Sūtra* 1.28, stating that mindful, contemplative repetition (*japa*) of the sacred syllable *oṁ*, is a practice of both *svādhyāya* and *Īśvara Pranidhāna*, and constitutes a "core practice" of yoga).

309. *The Telomere Effect* (reporting throughout the book the ways that attitudes and behaviors play a role in longevity).

310. *Flow*, at 104 (describing how *āsana* builds physical resiliency and *prāṇāyāma* relaxes the body and stabilizes breathing).

training for learning to direct our attention towards pursuit of any of the elements of wellbeing.

The fifth limb of *pratyāhāra*, sense withdrawal, is valuable for helping us refine our ability to avoid distraction. We learn through its practice to withdraw our senses inwards to remove ourselves from distraction. This ability is also important for better assimilating experiences our senses have presented to us and making choices. Let's say we meet somebody new or receive an invitation for something. This limb, with practice, gives us a freedom to better contemplate and consider how to respond to these experiences, how to weigh the pros and cons. This ability to withdraw the senses inward is also necessary if we are to remain on task, avoiding the temptations all around us. We learn to "see, hear, and feel only what one wishes to admit into awareness."[311] **This ability to immunize ourselves from outside distractions so that we can focus is vital for building the type of warm, supporting relationships that are a hallmark of wellbeing. Pause for a moment and remember what it feels like when somebody truly listens to you, really tries to "hear" you. It's a warm, embracing feeling, one that you can similarly evoke in others by your own empathetic listening. Learning to master your response to sensory distractions will help you develop and nurture relationships.**

The sixth limb of *dhāranā*, single-pointed focus, involves learning how to concentrate our attention.[312] This is the practice of sustained focus I've mentioned, with the point of concentration "either within or outside the body."[313] As we develop the ability to sustain our concentration in an uninterrupted way, we move into the seventh limb, *dhyāna*. This is the point that Patañjali refers to as the state of "meditation."[314] In this state of sustained concentration or meditation we "forget the self in uninterrupted

---

311. *Flow*, at 104.

312. *Flow*, at 105.

313. *Light on the Yoga Sūtras of Patañjali*, at 178–179 (describing *dhāranā* as a focus "on external or internal objects").

314. *Light on the Yoga Sūtras of Patañjali*, at 179–180 (commenting that the "characteristic feature of meditation" "is the maintenance of an uninterrupted flow of attention on a fixed point or region, without intervention or interruption").

concentration."[315] This state of mind occurs in full engagement, discussed in Chapter 3. We are so fully involved in the activity we lose our sense of anything other than engagement in the activity.

Patañjali's eighth limb is *samādhi*, meditative absorption. *Samādhi* has been referred to as a point at which "the meditator and the object of the meditation become as one...a joyous, self-forgetful involvement through concentration."[316] In *samādhi*, the uninterrupted "flow of attention dissolves the split between the object seen and the seer who sees it."[317] In terms of creating wellbeing, this is the moment when mental clarity and focus are rewarded through a connection to our experience such that we become totally absorbed in that experience, whether it is of a positive emotion, an engaging activity, a meaningful act, accomplishing a goal, or the warmth of a nurturing relationship.

315. *Flow*, at 105.

316. *Flow*, at 105.

317. *Light on the Yoga Sūtras of Patañjali*, at 181.

Meditation—a summary.

Meditation is a vital, essential practice for helping us develop the increased awareness, focus, and effective connection with ourselves we need to maximize wellbeing. Meditation, with steady practice, teaches us to master the movement of our thoughts. And when we practice all eight of Patañjali's limbs, we learn to more effectively connect with others by engaging in life habits and regulating instincts and desires that otherwise would interfere with that connection.[318]

Āsana—yoga poses.

Āsana, the third limb of Patañjali's *Yoga Sūtras*, refers to an appropriate seat for meditation as well as yoga postures or poses.[319] Millions of people around the world practice yoga poses every day for a variety of reasons—getting a workout, stretching, stress relief, healing an injury, and simply to feel good. **My purpose for discussing yoga poses here is to illustrate their value for increasing awareness, including self-awareness, sharpening focus, and as a method for developing our ability to more effectively connect with others.**

INCREASED AWARENESS.

Yoga poses increase our awareness by training us to direct our attention to what we are doing in every phase of the pose, including entering the pose and coming out of it. Why is paying attention throughout the pose so important? The human body has a general anatomical blueprint. Knees, shoulders, hips, the neck, the spine, and all other parts of the body are constructed to move in a certain way. Consider the knee joint, which in-

---

318. *Flow*, at 105–106 (describing how, collectively, the eight limbs make the "similarities between Yoga and flow...extremely strong").

319. *The Yoga Sūtras of Patañjali*, at 283–289 (commenting on *Yoga Sūtras* 2.46–2.48 pertaining to *āsana*).

cludes the thigh bone, patella, shinbone, tendons, ligaments, and cartilage. This joint is designed to allow movement in specific directions. Strains and tears can occur when we allow the knee to move outside the scope of that joint's design while performing a yoga pose. This can occur over time if we routinely practice certain poses with the knee joint out of proper alignment. Eventually that joint can become overstressed, perhaps through constantly over-stretching a medial or collateral ligament.

One pose in which yoga teachers see this type of injury is Warrior II, (*Vīrabhadrāsana* II). In the "full expression" of this pose—what it looks like in pictures modeling its final form—the front thigh is parallel to the floor, creating a 90-degree angle at the knee between the front calf and the thigh bone. The knee points directly forward, in line with the heel.[320] This is not easy to accomplish, and so a common instruction in an "alignment-based" class when encouraging the students to get a deeper bend in the front leg is to direct the student to lengthen from the inner groin out through the inner knee, and draw from the outer knee back through the outer front hip bone. This instruction is designed to help create a further bend in the front leg to bring the front thigh closer to parallel while at the same time keeping the knee correctly aligned. However, in cases in which a student has never heard this instruction, or has forgotten it, that student might develop the habit of regularly allowing the bent front knee to point inward or outward instead of straight ahead. Eventually, after being forced to bend deeper and deeper in this misaligned state, the knee is injured, and the student won't understand how that could have happened. To avoid such injuries, as well as to maximize the benefits of poses, we learn to maintain attention on the alignment of our anatomical blueprint throughout each pose. In this case, we learn to pay attention to the knee to make sure it moves in its proper direction, rather than being allowed to remain misaligned as force is directed through it.

---

320. *See Light on Yoga*, at 72.

This attention to detail will greatly increase our skill of awareness. As you can imagine, poses, such as Warrior II, require that we stay aware of a number of movements and actions in the body, not just the front knee.[321] We "initiate an action," such as lengthening out through the inner knee while drawing the outer knee back, "and somewhere else in the body, something else moves without your permission."[322] In Warrior II, for example, as we perform our front leg actions, quite often the trunk of the body begins to lean forward, out of its intended position perpendicular to the floor. We have to develop the ability to notice that change, ask ourselves if this change is "right or wrong? If wrong, what can I do to change it?"[323] And there are many other aspects to the pose that must be analyzed as well in order to create the outer form of a pose consistent with our anatomical blueprint. Only then can we expect to gain the full benefits available to us as we perform a pose.

To gain the full benefits offered by *āsana* practice, we learn to "align and harmonize" the physical body, using our breath as a pathway all the way to our core, our deepest, spiritual essence, ultimately achieving an integration of the entire self.[324] With enough proper practice, using our body to discipline the mind, our *āsana* practice can even become a "spiritual practice in action" as poses move us beyond an awareness of the body towards an awareness of the soul itself.[325]

---

321. In yoga poses, a "movement" and an "action" are different. A movement involves a change of position that puts the body into the outer form of the pose, such as "step your feet apart" or "bend your right knee towards 90 degrees." In contrast, an action involves application of some energy generated by countervailing forces to refine the pose, such as "root down through the outer heel of the back foot." Jones, Todd. "Illustrate Different Yoga Methods with Trikonāsana." *Yoga Journal*. August 28, 2007 (interview with John Schumacher); https://www.yogajournal.com/practice/the-right-triangle; retrieved January 5, 2019.

322. Iyengar, B.K.S. (2005). *Light on Life*. Emmaus, PA: Rodale, at 28.

323. *Light on Life*, at 28.

324. *Light on Life*, at 23, 27 (discussing how to perform a pose not "merely as a physical exercise but as a means to understand and then integrate our body with our breath, with our mind, with our intelligence, with our conscience, and with our core" so that we reach alignment and harmony through all layers of ourselves—the body, and our subtle emotional, mental, and spiritual body).

325. *Light on Life*, at 62–63 (describing how we might consider that "the body is the bow, *āsana* the arrow, and soul is the target"). B.K.S. Iyengar explained how we can learn to

To practice this way, to achieve this integration, we perform a pose in five stages, conative, cognitive, mental, emotional, and spiritual.[326] Employing these stages is an extraordinary practice for developing the skill of awareness. By practicing *āsana* with this "intensity of awareness" we learn to hold our attention on whatever we choose for so long as it serves us.[327] The attention required to perform a pose by applying all five of these stages refines our brain's ability to discriminate as we learn to weigh choices with a higher level of skill and intelligence.[328] Just as we learn in yoga practice to constantly assess if we are performing the pose in a way that optimizes its value to us, we take that same skill into life outside of yoga. We learn to ask the same questions of the choices we face in life—is this opportunity of value or not? Is what I'm about to say or do helpful to anyone or not? Am I going to build wellbeing or diminish it?

The first stage of a pose is called conative action. We begin a pose by paying attention to the physical movements and actions of our body, making sure we've placed our body in conformance with our anatomical blueprint. "Conative action is a purely physical response to what our mind tells the body to do."[329] Initially, when we first start doing yoga poses, we listen to an instruction from the teacher and then we direct our body to follow the instruction. Or, if we are learning to do yoga poses from a book, we ask our body to copy what we see in the pictures and read in the printed description. At some point we tap into our memory of what we know about a pose and our mind directs our body—"stretch the arms in opposite directions," "lift through the chest," or "root down through the back heel."

---

perform our poses by feeling "through love and devotion" instead of with our mind. *Light on Life*, at 63. He pointed out that a pose can become a devotional offering to God, *Īśvara Pranidhāna*. *Light on Life*, at 63.

326. *Light on the Yoga Sūtras of Patañjali*, at 158.

327. *Light on the Yoga Sūtras of Patañjali*, at 158–160 (describing how the intensity of awareness developed from practicing *āsana* leads the practitioner from single-pointed focus to a "non-specific attentiveness," opening the door to an experience of "unalloyed happiness, blessedness and beatitude").

328. *Light on Life* at 162 (discussing how *āsana* can cultivate our intelligence by teaching us, in the performance of the pose, how to discriminate between right and wrong action).

329. Iyengar, B.K.S. (2002 ed). *The Tree of Yoga*. Boston, MA: Shambhala Publications, Inc, at 47 (describing conative action as a physical action "at its most direct level," as the mind desires the body to do something and directs it to do so).

Our mind is telling the body parts what to do. As I've already explained in our example with Warrior II, that process in and of itself develops a high level of skill in paying attention.

The second stage of a pose is called cognitive action. This is when we feel the results of the action we've just taken.[330] We perceive the results with the body itself, by means of "the skin, eyes, nose and tongue—all our organs of perception."[331] Cognition allows us to pause in the moment and fully recognize what we've just done.[332] For example, in a Warrior II pose if I move my knee from its misaligned drift over the big toe into a straight ahead position consistent with the anatomical blueprint of the knee, I might suddenly feel something new—a knee that doesn't feel like I'm overstretching something! If I lift my chest towards the ceiling, I can feel my spine straightening. If I reach up fully towards the ceiling with straight, extended arms, I can feel not only the spine lengthening, I can feel my side body getting longer, space developing between the ribs and in the shoulder joints. This second stage offers us even more training of awareness because our attention moves from the most gross observations, such as the placement of the knee or chest, to a more subtle awareness, such as the increased space in a joint. We're scanning the body in search of such changes.

This leads to the third stage of the pose, the mental phase. Here the mind assimilates the feelings of our body, from the skin all the way down to the cellular level, arising from the actions we just took.[333] At this stage we use the "faculty of the mind" to assess and direct us to make any refinements to the pose necessary in order to perform the pose correctly.[334] If I extend my arms overhead and overstretch them just a wee bit, I might feel the beginning of stress on the fascia in the rib cage area, and so I back off. In my Wheel pose (*Ūrdhva Dhanurāsana*) I may notice that on this particular day, since I'm a bit more open and warmed up than usual,

---

330. *Light on the Yoga Sūtras of Patañjali*, at 158.

331. *The Tree of Yoga*, at 47.

332. *Light on Life*, at 126.

333. *The Tree of Yoga*, at 47 (describing how the mind, in what Mr. Iyengar calls the "communion" or "communication" stage of a pose, "introduces the intellect and connects it to every part of the body").

334. *Light on the Yoga Sūtras of Patañjali*, at 158.

I'm beginning to overstretch my abdominal muscles that I normally don't involve as much in this pose. So, I adjust. Or my teacher Mary comments that I'm not fully extending my arms overhead and, as my mind checks to see if that is the case, sure enough, I can straighten them more.

What we observe at this phase of the pose helps inform us not only of the manner in which we do the yoga pose, but also how we go about our lives. For example, we examine any pain or discomfort we might be experiencing in a pose to determine if it is caused by an unsafe overtaxing of the body. That analysis can reveal any number of things to us. Perhaps our ego is driving us to overextend so, out of a competitive urge, we seek to perform a pose as deeply as the guy next to us or to impress the teacher or somebody else in class. If that is the case, we can use that information to ask ourselves where else in our life we are letting our ego get in the way of our better judgment. How often do we push ourselves beyond a level that is reasonable just because of old habits of searching for approval from others or having to be perfect? Alternatively, maybe when we begin to feel discomfort in a pose, we tend to back off prematurely out of fear from an old injury. We know we are healed and sense we could take the pose a bit further, but we let fear get in the way. We might then ask ourselves how often we let our fears, or other patterns of thought and emotion, cause us to prematurely walk away from opportunities for greater wellbeing.

There are numerous other ways the mental phase of the pose informs us as to how we are approaching life. Maybe, as I mentioned earlier, I'm not straightening my arms completely when I lift them overhead because I'm feeling sad or lackluster, and that attitude is showing up in my life, causing me to isolate myself socially. The mental phase provides ongoing information we can use not only to perform poses safely but also take on life fully. In this way the mental phase of the pose is a great tool for assessing and recalibrating, if necessary, how much courage, tolerance, and tenacity we bring to life's challenges off the yoga mat, in our everyday life.[335]

---

335. *Light on Life*, at 47–48 (discussing how to examine discomfort associated with our yoga poses to determine what that discomfort teaches us about ourselves).

All of these refinements, all this attention to detail, are intended to move us into our optimal blueprint, our full expression of the pose. Hopefully, by now, you can see how this method of paying attention in our yoga practice is an incredibly effective way to train our skill of awareness so that we don't miss anything of value that life invites us to experience.

This gives rise to the fourth stage of a pose, the intellectual or reflective phase, in which we use our "discriminative mind" to observe and analyze the feelings of the pose throughout our body. We reflect on what we are experiencing in "the front, the back, the inside, and the outside," asking ourselves what we are feeling now that is new?[336] In Warrior II, for example, I feel a knee without pain. In my Upward Salute Pose (*Ūrdhva Hastāsana*), arms extended straight overhead in Mountain Pose, I feel a full, safe, lengthening of my spine and side body. As I feel these things physically, using my breath as a guide, emotions begin to arise. This happens because at this point the body and mind are working together in a process of "interweaving" "all the threads and fibers of our being."[337]

We've now reached the fifth and final stage of the pose, the spiritual stage. We've achieved the optimal alignment for our particular body on this particular day. For example, on this day, at this moment, my Warrior II, even with a front thigh that isn't parallel to the floor, has reached a stage in which I have a "firmness of body, steadiness of intelligence and benevolence of spirit."[338] I'm in proper alignment and my pose is now "steady and comfortable."[339] I'm not over-efforting because my ego isn't in charge, trying to force me into a deeper bend of the front leg. I know I'm expending appropriate effort, nothing less but nothing more, in reaching out from the inner groin to the inner knee and drawing from the outer knee back to the outer hip, without provoking a tear. I know that I'm still a nice person, a perfectly fine fellow even though there are others who can bend their leg

336. *The Tree of Yoga*, at 47.

337. *Light on Life*, at 30–31.

338. *Light on the Yoga Sūtras of Patañjali*, at 157–159 (translating Patañjali's *Yoga Sūtra* 2.46).

339. *The Yoga Sūtras of Patañjali*, at 283 (translating Patañjali's *Yoga Sūtra* 2.46).

more. For me, I've now achieved "perfection" in the pose, and "the infinite being within" me is accessible.[340] What does that mean?

In this fifth, or spiritual stage of the pose, we achieve "a total awareness, from the self to the skin and from the skin to the self," a total integration of mind, body, and spirit.[341] We experience a sense of benevolence and intelligence in our mind, and a feeling of joyous and deep self-awareness in our heart.[342] For example, at this stage I might feel powerful in this properly aligned, full expressions of the pose. There is an extraordinary feeling of confidence when I extend out fully in Warrior II pose, my body optimally aligned so I can tap into all my power and direct it forward, into the future, metaphorically, as I gaze over my extended front hand. At the same time, I honor my past as my back hand fully extends backward, my upper body perpendicular to the floor. That feeling isn't fully available when a part of my body is misaligned, sending my mind nagging interference, like the static on a slightly mistuned radio. At some level the mind knows that something is off, there's a fuller expression yet untouched. But, in this fifth stage that static isn't there; the mind knows that everything is finely tuned. So, I feel confident, excited about my future, grateful for my past, ready to take some risks to express my potential. And with these emotions moving through me, I feel aligned with something bigger than me—with life and all the other people out there trying to live their best life, provide for their families, and achieve their own wellbeing. In this fifth stage I've tapped into my highest nature, a subject I discuss more fully in Chapter 10.

USE OF PROPS.

Regardless of our particular level of *āsana* practice, health and physical condition, flexibility, strength, and individual physical anomalies, there

---

340. *Light on the Yoga Sūtras of Patañjali*, at 159–160 (translating Patañjali's *Yoga Sūtra* 2.47).

341. *The Tree of Yoga*, at 47.

342. *Light on the Yoga Sūtras of Patañjali*, at 157–158 (commenting on *Yoga Sūtra* 2.46).

is a very good chance that we could benefit from the use of yoga props.[343] Yoga props are "any object that helps stretch, strengthen, relax, or improve the alignment" of our particular body in a pose.[344] Props include walls, chairs, blocks, ropes suspended from a wall, straps, benches of various sizes and shapes, bolsters, and blankets, by way of example. Props help us position our body into the proper form of a pose. Once we attain the proper form of the pose, aided as needed by props, we are better able to focus our mind on the pose itself because we are not distracted by over-efforting, fatigue, or stresses we might be otherwise placing on our body and mind by being out of alignment. Props also help us build our strength and endurance by allowing us to remain in a pose, in proper alignment, for a longer period of time than we might otherwise be able to sustain. We are then able to study the actions of the pose more carefully and feel the body and mind's feedback, then respond to that feedback by making any necessary adjustments.

Let me give you a few examples from my own practice. Due to some neck injuries (not from yoga, by the way), I no longer bear weight on my head, which means that headstands (*Sālamba Śīrṣāsana*) would be out of the question but for props. As a result, I've learned various alternative methods of inverting into a form of headstand that doesn't put weight on my head. Sometimes I use two chairs facing each other at a wall, placing some blankets on the seats to support my shoulders. Then, with my head extending towards the floor in the space between the two chairs, I lift my legs overhead. Other times I use short stacks of blocks to support my shoulders, my hands on the floor or blocks (*Śīrṣāsana* II or Tripod headstand). Or, as another alternative, I hang upside down using ropes affixed to the wall. In each of these cases I'm able to access many of the benefits of this pose, such as increased relaxation, but without putting pressure on my cervical spine. I can take time to feel if any part of my body needs an adjusting action and then make the adjustments without putting any pressure on my head.

As another example of how I use props, I frequently sit on chairs to

343. Iyengar, B.K.S. (2001). *Yoga The Path to Holistic Health*. London, England: Dorling Kindersley Limited, at 164–167 (discussing performance of poses with props and identifying various common props).

344. *Yoga The Path to Holistic Health*, at 164.

help with twisting poses, using the arms and seat of the chair to help push or pull my body into an additional range of motion. In addition, I regularly use chairs and blocks to help me with my backbends, sometimes putting my feet on the seat of the chair to direct more focus to my upper spine area. Other times I place my hands onto the chair or onto blocks to help me lift off the floor to press my chest towards the ceiling. I sit on blankets to help put my lower back into an optimal position when doing seated poses. And I use blocks to help me attain a full expression of certain standing poses, such as Triangle pose (*Trikonāsana*), when my hand can't quite reach the floor without pulling my upper body into a contracted, downward-facing position, a limiting position for the upper body in that particular pose.

These are just a few examples from my own practice. **Whether we use walls to help check our posture, blankets to help achieve a proper lumbar curve, chairs to assist us in balancing on one leg, or any number of other alternatives, props are a tremendous aid to us as we use *āsana* practice to increase our awareness.** Each time we reach for a prop we are practicing the important habit of setting aside that part of our ego that might, if unchecked, interfere with our efforts to build wellbeing. Just as we might use a chair or blocks to help us get into a healthy backbend instead of trying to force our spine into position, so, too, we learn not to force our opinions on others as we seek to build connection with them. By taking a moment or two in our *āsana* practice to truly feel the effects of a properly-aligned pose, we are also learning how to pause throughout our day to notice and appreciate the wonders of being alive. The use of props encourages us to become aware of everything we feel and everything we think—a skill we require to maximize wellbeing.

INCREASED FOCUS.

Performing poses with proper attention to alignment also increases our ability to focus. During the pose we focus on maintaining our alignment, even as we adjust various parts of the body, to make sure we don't "distort" our body's "normal or original structure."[345] We focus to make sure the

---

345. Iyengar, B.K.S. (2012). *Core of the Yoga Sūtras*. London, ENG: HarperThorsens, at 148.

joints and muscles are "kept in their natural shape and form" by directing a "single-focused" attention to the entire body, maintaining that alignment, but making refinements to the alignment as needed.[346] We use our mind and intelligence to pay attention to every joint, bone, muscle, fiber, ligament, tendon, and cell in a "focused awareness" that we feel "in every particle of the body."[347]

As I mentioned earlier, when we are doing a pose, we might find that as we move one part of the body into proper alignment, another part of the body moves out of its optimal anatomical blueprint. For example, again using our Warrior II pose, we move the knee into its proper position on the front, bent leg. However, as soon as we turn our attention away from the knee and direct that attention towards the upper body to keep it from leaning forward, the front knee drifts over the big toe again. And, while that is going on, the two arms, extended in opposite directions, move out of plane from each other, one towards the ceiling and one towards the floor. To deal with this, we have to develop a "single-focused grip" on those parts of the body that are properly aligned. Then, "observing and feeling this single-focused grip," we keep that grip on the part of the body we just adjusted and turn our attention to the rest of the body to get it into the proper, safe position.[348] In our Warrior II pose we keep a focus on the front knee, and holding that focus, we then realign the upper body so it is perpendicular to the floor, attaching a single-focused grip onto that as well. We then direct our attention to our arms, bringing them both parallel to the floor, reaching equally in opposite directions.

It is easy to see that if a person practices yoga poses this way, particularly if they have a teacher pointing out misalignments to them, before long, it eventually becomes easier to use our increased skill of focus to pay attention to our partner or friend at dinner even though all sorts of interesting people are walking back and forth past the table. Off the yoga mat we don't have to be focusing on all our different body parts like we

---

346. *Core of the Yoga Sūtras*, at 148–149 (describing how to focus in order to continually refine alignment in a pose).

347. *Core of the Yoga Sūtras*, at 148.

348. *Core of the Yoga Sūtras*, at 148–149 (describing how we must learn a single-focused grip so we can adjust other parts of the body).

do performing a pose, we just have to pay attention to one human being. Obviously, developing this level of skill of sustaining focus makes it much less of a challenge to maintain our concentration on tasks we undertake to accomplish something important to us. Distractions no longer interfere.

MORE EFFECTIVE CONNECTION.

With proper practice, yoga poses invite us to a deeper connection to the emotional and spiritual self. Master yoga teacher Geeta Iyengar wrote that yoga poses "take one from the physical to the spiritual plane."[349] As we turn our attention inward, we begin to experience whatever arises in the pose. The pose becomes a way to "investigate meditatively deep and subtle feelings, responses, and reflexes."[350] In this process of going inward, we synchronize "all aspects of our mind or psyche."[351] At some point the pose becomes an "active meditation" in which we can find a "oneness of body, mind, and soul."[352] This is a wonderful reward of practicing *āsana*; as we become increasingly skilled in our practice of *āsana*, we experience ever deepening levels of insight into our self, penetrating to the core of our being.[353] With this insight we learn how to regularly connect with our hopes, dreams, desires, goals, and as yet untapped potential. And as we will see in Chapter 10, proficiency in taking this inward journey gives us ready access to our highest nature as a human being, the most profoundly magnificent version of ourselves.

I've already described the process through which this inward journey can occur and even offered an example of how a full expression in a pose can generate emotional and spiritual benefits. I now want to briefly elab-

---

349. Iyengar, Getta (1990). *Yoga A Gem for Women*. Spokane, WA: Timeless Books, at 25.

350. Freeman, Richard (2010). *The Mirror of Yoga*. Boston, MA: Shambhala Publications, at 1.

351. Feuerstein, Dr. Georg (2007). *Yoga Morality*. Prescott, AZ: Hohm Press, at 39-40.

352. *The Tree of Yoga*, at 149.

353. *The Mirror of Yoga*, at 10–12 (discussing how a person can understand and experience the interconnectedness of all things through the merger of mind and body in a single pose). *See also Inside the Yoga Sūtras*, at 20–21 (commenting that a pose can be a vehicle beneficial to our growth as a human being).

orate on this process, describing some of what we might expect to find on our inward journey from the physical to the spiritual plane. First, there are numerous physical benefits from performing poses. When we set the foundation of a pose, such as standing at the top of our mat in Mountain Pose (*Tādāsana*), we relax our body, releasing bodily tension as we calm our breath. We then scan our body and make any adjustments we need to bring our body into its anatomical blueprint. Perhaps there is an uneven distribution of our weight on one foot as opposed to the other, maybe one foot is turned out instead of pointing straight ahead, and possibly the knees are bent. We may notice that the tops of our upper thigh bones are forward of the knees, causing our upper body to lean backward or perhaps forward. We correct that by bringing the top of the thigh bones back under the hips. When we do this, we see that our upper body is still leaning, maybe even more so, one way or another, and so we make adjustments to that. We straighten the arms, turn the palms to face each other, noticing that one palm was pointing in a different direction than the other. We note that and check in with the shoulder on that arm to see if that is playing a role in the hand position. We then adjust, perhaps by relaxing a tense pectoralis minor or anterior (front) deltoid muscle. Next, we feel where the head is in relation to the spine. Does it need to be drawn back?

If you don't practice yoga, you may not realize that what I've just listed is only part of a checklist an experienced practitioner attends to in Mountain Pose just at the very beginning. And the checklist will vary, depending on what the practitioner did that day. Maybe an ankle is slightly sprained from a hike, or the "computer/mouse" shoulder is particularly tight because of heavy computer work that day. Continuing with Mountain Pose as our example, there is also much to observe in the back of the body, making sure the low back has a proper curve, before beginning to apply any effort to lengthen the spine. If we don't bring the lower back into a proper curve, any force moving through the low back will aggravate its narrowed, compressed state, possibly leading to pain and injury.

Over time, with proper practice, a practitioner can do this scan in the moment, and, even then, it is not unusual that there will still be something to adjust. All of this attentiveness, across the entire range of the body, from the breath to the skin, while paying attention to the teacher's instructions or our own memory of what is optimal, is very beneficial mentally. **Prac-**

ticing poses with this level of awareness, constantly directing the mind towards various parts of the body, builds mental clarity, enhanced perceptivity and discriminatory awareness. This process even develops our creativity as, for example, we ponder in the moment how to redistribute our weight evenly on both feet. After my hip replacement I regularly noticed that the weight on my right foot drifted to the outer edge. I had to think about what was going on in my body to cause that, remembering that the muscles and fascia on the upper inner right thigh had been traumatized in the surgery and were tight. So, I'd draw my right leg up a bit more strongly into the socket, creating room for the new femur head to move subtlety just enough so I could broaden the back of my right thigh in order to then evenly distribute weight on the right foot. That is quite a bit of attention and analysis and we're not five seconds into the beginning of the pose! Of course, years of practice with great teachers helps.

I give you these examples to help illustrate how performing a yoga pose is such an incredibly effective means for developing the mental clarity we need, the skill of awareness, to maximize our wellbeing. If you can pay attention to which part of your right foot is carrying extra weight, you will be far more likely not only to awaken to your own internal voice—your power, as well as your hopes and dreams—but you will also be better able to spot a warm, inviting smile from a stranger or catch the beautiful sunsets of life that often only seem to appear to others.

I've barely touched the surface of the physical benefits of performing a pose. We certain build strength and endurance in our body, as well as increased flexibility. However, there are also emotional benefits. We might experience a sense of freedom. That might seem odd, given how much structure I am talking about in terms of body placement and mental acuity. Let me give you an example. I developed a habit of turning my right foot out in mountain pose instead of pointing it straight ahead. I did this in every Mountain pose, every class, and at every workshop or retreat, despite teachers telling me to correct it. In other words, I did it a lot. Not surprisingly, I had lower back pain. Eventually I figured out where the pain was coming from. When I stood in Mountain Pose with my left foot straight, but my right foot pointed out, and then applied effort to lengthen my spine upwards from that base, I was pinching my sacroiliac joint on the right, compressing a major nerve. I was strong and, having practiced quite a bit, could exert some real power into that misaligned joint as I continually compressed it. Figuring this out, I then found that when I adjusted my foot to point straight ahead, the pain subsided because that joint widened back to its natural position, freeing the nerve from the constriction. I asked my friend Dennis, a yoga therapist, to stand behind me whenever we did a class together so he could remind me to point my foot straight ahead. He was kind enough to do so and helped me change my habit. Thanks Dennis! It was an amazing feeling of freedom to then be able to fully lengthen through that pose, pain-free. I could open my chest, expand my rib cage, and, no longer distracted by pain, feel the power inherent in that pose. I could feel the stability from which Mountain pose gets its name. These feelings brought with them not only the sense of freedom I mentioned, but also emotions such as confidence, equanimity, tranquility, and a general sense of letting go. Every one of these emotional benefits help us off the mat outside the yoga studio as we seek to more effectively connect with others and with life, in our pursuit of wellbeing.

We can even experience spiritual benefits just from setting a proper foundation in a pose. In Mountain pose, for example, once we are properly aligned, spine straight and chest lifting, we may experience a sense of our connection to something bigger than just ourselves, a deeply-rooted knowledge that we are all connected to each other in our shared desire to feel good, safe, optimistic, and free to pursue our dreams. Feeling firmly supported as we stand on the mat, facing forward, the heart area open, breath moving evenly, and fully aware, it is here that we might catch a glimpse of our unlimited potential. All this, and more, can occur simply by pausing long enough, not much more than "a blink of the eye" to move all the way from the outer body into our essence.

So far, I've only discussed the possibilities available to us while establishing the basic foundation of a pose, such as Mountain pose. Once we actually begin to perform the pose there is the opportunity for experiencing a wealth of additional benefits.[354] In Mountain pose, like any pose, the

---

354. For an excellent and thorough discussion of the landscape of this inner journey, the *kośas*, also referred to as *koshas*, or "Sheaths of Being," *see Light on Life*, in which Mr. Iyengar provided a detailed description of the experiences possible as we move back and forth between our physical body, *annamaya kośa*, and our "soul body," *ānandamaya kośa* (also discussing *prāṇāmaya kośa*, our energetic body, *manomaya kośa*, our mental body, and *vijñānamaya kośa*, our intellectual body). And for another explanation of these sheaths

ultimate goal of doing the pose is to perform it by extending and expand-ing "from the core of your being" out "dynamically in all directions."[355] In Mountain pose, then, we lengthen through our spine all the way out to the top of the head (and, energetically, beyond). We apply just the right amount of energy so that the pose becomes a full expression of us—a mind, body, and spirit proclamation of who we are and all that we are experiencing at that moment.

There are physical benefits of this full expression, such as creating space in the joints, aligning the skeleton, increasing range of motion, increasing circulation, and increasing oxygen intake. There are mental benefits as well. These include release of tension and focusing of our thoughts. From these might arise emotional benefits such as an expression of commitment, freedom, and courage, as well as a sense of personal power. And spiritual benefits may also arise, including what we've emphasized so much in this book, an unbridled joyous expression of our potential, manifested through our body, mind, and spirit, in this single pose.[356]

ĀSANA AS AN ACTIVE MEDITATION.

As you can now see, *āsana* can serve as an active meditation, allowing us to connect to our emotional and spiritual core. Let's look at how we do a pose in terms of Patañjali's methodology for meditation, discussed earlier. First, as we do the pose, we can't be gazing all over the room or out the window. We shouldn't be thinking about what to make for dinner or who might be at the party later that night. Rather, we're directing close attention to the body, the breath, and whatever feelings our actions evoke. We "withdraw our attention from outward objects by directing the input of our senses"

---

through use of stories from everyday life, consider *Finding the Midline*, at 178–203.

355. *Light on Life*, at 33 (explaining that this extension is in fact an expansion as well, occurring in all directions) .

356. Of course, after setting the proper foundation for the pose, there are additional steps to take to ensure proper alignment before fully extending out in the pose. These steps include proper integration of the body, such as the joints and muscle insertions and attachments, as well as creating proper curvature in the spine. There are physical, mental, emotional, and spiritual benefits possible during these steps as well.

as we focus on the pose.[357] This withdrawing of the senses away from distractions is *pratyāhāra*, the fifth limb of Patañjali's yoga.

However, as we are withdrawing the senses, we sustain focus on all parts of the body relative to each other. We "shift the light of awareness," refining the pose as we seek optimal alignment.[358] We control the fluctuations of our mind, drawing all our focus to an ever-increasing refinement of the pose.[359] We are not yet meditating; we are concentrating our attention. This concentration is *dhāranā*, the sixth limb of the eight-limbed path of Patañjali's yoga.[360] When we are able to maintain this attention "without altering or wavering in the intensity of awareness," we've moved from *dhāranā* to *dhyāna*, which is meditation.[361] As we sustain this unwavering concentration on the entire body, the breath, the mind, emotions, and spirit, we may reach a state of equanimity "wherein the feeling of effort disappears" and we enjoy the pleasure of a fully unified body, mind, and spirit.[362] This is full absorption in the pose, *samādhi*, the eighth limb.[363]

ĀSANA—A SUMMARY.

The benefits that come from practicing poses with attention and focus on alignment will unfold the more we practice and will become more and more accessible as we practice "uninterruptedly and with devotion over a prolonged period of time."[364] Performing yoga poses this way develops the

---

357. *Flow*, at 104.

358. *The Tree of Yoga*, at 43.

359. *The Tree of Yoga*, at 139 (describing how our attention becomes focused "within or outside the body," gradually decreasing fluctuations of the mind until the practitioner and the pose merge into one).

360. *Light on the Yoga Sūtras of Patañjali*, at 158 (commenting on Patañjali's *Yoga Sūtra* 2.46).

361. *The Tree of Yoga*, at 139.

362. *Core of the Yoga Sūtras*, at 152.

363. *The Tree of Yoga*, at 72–77 (commenting that diffusing consciousness through the body and all its parts, using our intelligence as a "bridge between the soul and the body, creating the "divine union" of *samādhi*).

364. *The Yoga Sūtras of Patañjali*, at 49 (commenting on Patañjali's *Yoga Sūtra* 1.14). By

critical skills of awareness, focus, and increased effectiveness in connecting to ourselves—skills necessary to maximize wellbeing. This type of mindful yoga practice, regardless of the practitioner's particular style of yoga, increases our ability to recognize, embrace, and express ourselves fully in the world, to truly be the best we can be. And, of course, by developing these skills we become far more effective in creating positive relationship with others.

Prāṇāyāma.

For over two thousand years people all over the world have used some form of mindfulness practice, such as meditation, yoga, and *Tai Chi*, to create wellbeing.[365] Each of these practices emphasize attention to the breath. As I discussed earlier, research demonstrates that concentration on our breath is an excellent way to increase our awareness and ability to focus on the moment. Concentration on the breath helps prevent us from being distracted by the "constant stream of wayward thoughts" that get in the way of our fully experiencing life and building wellbeing.[366]

With practice, focus on the breath not only builds awareness, but it also builds "a self-regulatory mind-monitoring process that ultimately is an awareness of awareness itself."[367] This "awareness of awareness" can become a habit, eventually allowing us to view our own thoughts as they arise without judgment.[368]

---

using the term discussing "alignment" I don't intend to suggest that alignment-based styles of yoga are the only way to learn and practice yoga. There are tremendous teachers and practitioners in the styles of yoga known more for dynamic movement. As best as I can tell from my own experience, each of them, however, practice and teach proper alignment).

365. *Mindsight*, at 89.

366. Siegel, Dr. Daniel J. (2007). *The Mindful Brain*. New York, NY: W.W. Norton & Company, Inc., at 55.

367. *The Mindful Brain*, at 98.

368. *The Mindful Brain*, at 98.

Imagine how valuable such a skill can be in dealing with our patterns of thought and emotion. For example, we meet a new person and immediately we feel an old pattern of feeling unworthy. With the greater awareness we've developed through practices such as concentration on the breath, we immediately recognize that the old feeling is just that, something from the past that doesn't have anything to do with the present opportunity. Instead of giving in to the feeling of being unworthy, we simply acknowledge it and proceed to put our best foot forward in meeting that new person. We pay attention to learning about them instead of listening to our pesky voice from the past. In fact, we can teach ourselves to use the feeling of unworthiness as a cue to pay extra close attention to the person and what they have to say, what they have to offer. We turn the focus in this case outward towards that person instead of inwards towards the unhelpful feeling. We can learn to use attention to our breath as a means for this transformation of focus.

Focus on the breath is a common form of meditation practice, and, as I mentioned in our discussion of *āsana*, we learn to work with the breath while we do our yoga poses. However, *āsana* is not the only yoga practice in which attention to the breath is taught. Yoga also includes a particular area of practice directed towards building greater respiratory effectiveness as well as developing an increased ability to pay attention and maintain a sustained focus through the breath. That practice is *prāṇāyāma*, the fourth limb of Patañjali's eight-limb path of yoga.

The term *"prāna"* means "breath."[369] *"Āyāma"* means to "stretch" or "regulate."[370] Thus, *prāṇāyāma* is "breath control," the "regulation of the incoming and outgoing breaths."[371] In yoga, the regulation of breath in *prāṇ āyāma* practice includes various methods of prolonged inhalation, exhalation, and retention of the breath and also methods intended to direct the

369. *Prāna* also refers to our vital life force. This life force, according to yoga philosophy, sustains the existence of the world, including human beings. Iyengar, B.K.S. (2011 ed). *Light on Prāṇāyāma*. India: HarperCollins Publishers India, at 12. The life force of *prāna* is called *qi* or *chi* in Chinese practices, as in *qi gong* or *tai chi*, and *ki* in Japanese.

370. *Light on Prāṇāyāma*, at 13.

371. *The Yoga Sūtras of Patañjali*, at 289 (Dr. Bryant's commentary on Patañjali's *Yoga Sūtra* 2.49).

respiratory organs to move and expand in specific ways.[372] When practiced properly, the breathing exercises of *prāṇāyāma* increase our body's capacity to utilize the breath. The practices include horizontal expansion, vertical ascension, and circumferential extension of the lungs and the rib cage,[373] bringing "mobility and elasticity to the diaphragm."[374]

These exercises develop our ability to pay attention and focus.[375] They do so by directing our attention in very subtle ways as we "acutely sense and feel the movement of the breath."[376] We also pay attention to movements of the body in the area of the rib cage. The breathing exercises of *prāṇāyāma* use various techniques and ratios of inhalation, exhalation, and retention pacing in relationship with each other in order to "give us as many different possibilities for following the breath" as possible so that the mind learns to become drawn to the breath.[377] Thoughts are arrested as the mind becomes focused solely on the particular exercise. [378]

From my experience, a person unfamiliar with the practice of *prā.nāyāma* should consult with a teacher trained and experienced in teaching *prāṇāyāma* before beginning a practice. The teacher can assess whether the student's body is ready for the breathing practices and, if so, teach the student preparatory poses so that the body is opened up prior to beginning a *prāṇāyāma* practice. In this way the teacher can assure that the student is doing the exercises properly and without strain or risk of injury.

---

372. *The Yoga Sūtras of Patañjali*, at 290–291 (commenting on Patañjali's *Yoga Sūtra* 2.50).

373. *Light on Prāṇāyāma*, at 14 (describing actions in *prāṇāyāma* practice).

374. Iyengar, B.K.S. (2016). "Why should we practice *prāṇāyāma*?" In (Mehta, Rajvi H. ed). *Yoga Rahasya* (Vol. 23, No.1), Mumbai, Yog, at 4.

375. *Light on Pranayama*, at 14 (commenting that using the techniques of *prāṇāyāma* "helps the mind to concentrate and enables the *sādhaka* [practitioner] to attain robust health and longevity").

376. Desikachar, T.K.V. (1995). *The Heart of Yoga*. Rochester, VT: Inner Traditions International, at 56.

377. *The Heart of Yoga*, at 56.

378. *The Yoga Sūtras of Patañjali*, at 290 (commenting on Patañjali's *Yoga Sūtra* 2.49).

While there is much more to say about these and other yoga practices, this chapter is intended only as an introduction to some of the most common yoga practices and how they can be utilized for building wellbeing. Now, let's look at how the study of yoga philosophy assists us in more fully connecting to ourselves and with others.

Chapter 10
Yoga philosophy

Yoga practices, such as meditation, *āsana*, and *prāṇāyāma*, help us build the skills of awareness, focus, and more effective connection with ourselves and others, all critical to maximizing wellbeing. **However, to truly realize our highest potential as a human being, yoga philosophy offers us even more. It shows us our highest nature, those attributes existing within each human being that, when we choose to manifest them, transform us into the profoundly magnificent version of ourselves we can be.** In this final chapter I provide an overview of those attributes. In addition, I also describe time-proven standards we can learn from a study of yoga philosophy to guide us towards living in greater harmony with others.

Our highest nature.

In order to satisfy our central need of full self-expression and to experience the deep, self-affirming satisfaction that comes with that expression, we must learn to recognize and embrace our deepest essence as a human being.[379] This means that we go beyond just learning our strengths and drawing upon what we've learned throughout our life. We also need to recognize and live as the highest expression of what a human being is capable of being. We become somebody who by our very manner of living inspires others towards their own higher nature. In terms of wellbeing, we become meaningful every moment not only with what we do, but by the inspiring example we set in doing it.

---

379. *The Discovery of Being*, at 79–83 (referencing Nietzsche, Dr. May wrote "bringing one's inner potentialities into birth in action is the central dynamic and need of life").

To recognize this deepest essence within us, we can look to the nondual tantric traditions I mentioned in Chapter 8. Because they saw each of us as a living manifestation of the divine, Ultimate Reality, and sought to experience that imprint of divinity within themselves and others, they developed a set of personal attributes to help identify what that imprint looked like—what to look for. These attributes constituted the "true nature" of that Ultimate Reality, and, thus, the true nature of themselves and others.

I refer to these attributes as our "highest nature," what we can aspire to be as human beings. Just as the nondual tantric traditions ascribed these attributes to Ultimate Reality—so they could more readily identify and then connect to that divine nature within themselves, as well as in others—we too can utilize this information to realize our full potential as well as to build nurturing relationship with others. Regardless of our religious or spiritual beliefs, understanding these attributes, what these nondual tantric traditions view as our highest potential, offers us a guide for living life as the most profoundly magnificent version of ourselves possible.

We desire to fully know and express ourselves.

One of the oldest texts that forms part of the foundation of many yoga traditions is the *Ṛg Veda*. It is one of the four *Vedas* that, together, constitute the "earliest and most treasured scriptures of Hinduism."[380] Its "creation hymn" (10:129), described a power who created the world out of a burning desire to manifest itself, to fully know itself[381] According to the hymn, nothing existed at first but, out of a dark void of nothingness emerged the "One," an Ultimate Reality, pure Consciousness, filled with a passion to

---

380. *The Yoga Tradition*, at 27. The *Vedas* include collections of hymns and chants, methods for conducting rituals, and discussion of philosophy. They form the foundation for much of the law in India today regarding social, legal, domestic and religious customs and behavior. The *Ṛg Veda*, "which is to the pious Hindu what the Old Testament is to the Christian," *The Yoga Tradition*, at 6, is believed to be the oldest of the four *Vedas*, and is often dated somewhere around 1500 B.C.E. *The Yoga Tradition*, at 93–101 (suggesting approximate time period for *Ṛg Veda*). As with much of the references to yoga texts, dating any work of this type is subject to reasoned scholarly debate.

381. Doniger, Dr. Wendy (1991). *The Rig Veda*. New York, NY: Penguin Group, at 25–26.

exist, to manifest, to be.[382] From a nondual tantric perspective, we share that burning desire to fully know ourselves. As we've discussed as a main theme in this book, we know that this same desire drives each of us as a human being.

We are benevolent and kind.

The name given to Ultimate Reality by certain nondual traditions, *Paramśiva*, provides additional insight into our highest nature.[383] "*Parama*" means "supreme" and "*Śiva*" means "the Lord; the Auspicious One."[384] The word "auspicious" refers to a person, a thing, or an act suggesting success or attended by good fortune or prosperity.[385] Therefore, *Paramśiva* is associated with "prosperity," "well-being," "power," and "life-giving." For these reasons, the desire to give life and wellbeing to all of creation, *Paramśiva* is traditionally associated with benevolence and kindness.[386]

Because, according to this and some other yoga traditions, we share these characteristics with Ultimate Reality, **our highest nature, what we are capable of being, is also benevolent, kind, and creative, with a desire to contribute to creating a life of success and wellbeing for everyone.** This benevolence, the desire to create more wellbeing not only for ourselves but for others as well, is consistent with our discussion throughout this book that our greatest joy as a human being is to fully express ourselves by

---

382. The *Rig Veda*, at 25–26.

383. Somewhere around the ninth or tenth century, C.E., the nondual tantric Pratyabhi-jñā school of Kashmir Shaivism developed a thirty-six-category metaphysical cosmological model of the *Tattvas*, the categories of existence I referred to in Chapter 8. "Pratyabhijñā," means "recognizing" or "remembering," and refers to the process of recognizing that we are not separate from each other but, rather, all part of a single "infinite Reality." *The Yoga Tradition*, at 267. *Paramśiva* is the name they give to Ultimate Reality.

384. Shantananda, Swami (2003). *The Splendor of Recognition*. South Fallsburg, NY: SYDA Foundation, at 16.

385. Definition of "Auspicious." This link is directed to an online dictionary definition: https://www.merriam-webster.com/dictionary/auspicious; retrieved January 2, 2019.

386. *The Splendor of Recognition*, at 16 (describing *Paramśiva* as being associated with traits such as kindness, friendliness, and "the highest source of benevolence").

adding value to the world.[387] Our most "profound meaning and purpose," our most "indescribable joy," our "single most reliable momentary increase in well-being" arises from our interaction with others out of kindness.[388] And we know from the seventy-plus year Harvard study of behavior that "the most important contributor to joy and happiness in adult life is love,"[389] those times in which we resonate with other human beings in a positive way. It is no wonder that over a thousand years ago this group of yoga philosophers identified benevolence, kindness, and investment in each other's wellbeing as part of our highest human nature.

We have the power to create wellbeing for others.

In the metaphysical model I mentioned, *Paramśiva* consists of both a masculine energy, *Śiva*, and a feminine energy, *Śakti*. *Śiva* and *Śakti* work together to inspire and create the material world. *Śiva* is viewed as a shining light of potential, illuminating all that is possible, all that could be. *Śakti* is considered a creative energy, reflecting back the potential illuminated by *Śiva*'s light. This reflection makes him aware of what is possible. Through this process of "self-reflection," they first envision, and then create, each diverse form on our planet.[390]

This is an amazingly powerful metaphor to keep in mind as we contemplate how to create more relationship and meaning, how to experience and share positive emotions. The illuminating and reflective creative interaction between *Śiva* and *Śakti* is available to us. **We can use our own power of self-reflection to illuminate our own potential and then express**

387. *The Discovery of Being*, at 80–83 (stating that the satisfaction of our primal desire to be everything we are capable of being is a self-affirming feeling of power, considered the "essence of joy"); *see also Man's Search for Himself*, at 96 (writing that when we recognize that we've created something meaningful, we experience the gratification of affirming that we are a person "of worth and dignity").

388. *Flourish*, at 20 (describing the value of warm connections with others).

389. *Triumphs of Experience*, at 370.

390. *The Triadic Heart of Śiva*, at 95–99; *see also The Splendor of Recognition*, at 31–32. This interaction between *Śiva* and *Śakti* involves *prakāśa* (the shining forth of the light of pure Consciousness) and *vimarśa* (the power of reflection). *Splendor of Recognition*, at 27–33.

it, creating the life we want. Similarly, we engage in this creative process with others by searching for their potential, reflecting it back to them, and then coaxing them to bring that potential into action. In this way, we have, through interaction with another, produced something that otherwise would not exist—a more "realized" human being.

Sat—our personal wellspring.

Another attribute is *sat*. *Sat* means "Being,"[391] the Ultimate Reality,[392] and "eternal Truth."[393] Although we, as humans beings, are not eternal, we nonetheless have our own personal "truth." This truth consists of all the things I've mentioned previously—our character strengths, our life experiences, education, training—our general knowledge. Absent infirmity, this personal history, our particular truth, never leaves us, although we might forget some of it from time to time. This personal history serves as a wellspring we can draw upon whenever we choose and for whatever purpose.[394]

Chit—our self-awareness.

Another attribute is *chit*. *Chit* refers to our power of self-awareness, the ability to "understand," "perceive," or "know," our self.[395] **We have the ability to be fully self-aware of our unique "truth"—our potential. One of the values of practices such as meditation and *āsana* is that it develops a practice of self-study. Just as we learn to ask ourselves if the right knee**

---

391. *Auspicious Wisdom*, at 115.

392. *The Yoga Tradition*, at 459.

393. Mahony, Dr. William K. (2010). *Exquisite Love*. The Woodlands, TX: Anusara Press, at 20.

394. Kempton, Sally (2002). *Meditation for the Love of It*. Boulder, CO: Sounds True, Inc., at 36–37.

395. *The Splendor of Recognition*, at 25–26 (writing that in order to understand the "highest Reality," we have to first understand our self because we are each the doorway to that Reality).

feels like it is lined up correctly in Warrior II, we use that same ability to "go inward" to engage in a dialogue with ourselves to recognize what we have to offer in any given situation.

Ānanda—our capacity to experience the joy of creation.

Ānanda is described as a blissful feeling, a joy that comes from creating.[396] The joy arises out of the impulse to create for the pure delight of it.[397] It is out of this impulse that our world was created, according to the metaphysical theory of creation we've been referring to in this chapter.[398] We have the capacity to experience joy when we create. This feeling of joy can occur through accomplishing a goal, but it has added spice when we create something of value and meaning to the world through that accomplishment.

There are innumerable ways for us to experience the joy of creation. For example, recall our discussion in Chapter 2 about positivity resonance, our ability to share positive emotions with others. When we do so, we can literally transform another's mood from melancholy to amusement, from anger to gratitude, or from loneliness to a feeling of warm, nurturing connection. We experience the joyous act of creation whenever we help coax into the world another human's possibilities, getting somebody to laugh and feel better, helping another experience a sense of dignity in a moment of embarrassment, or any other way we act out of our highest nature to be kind.

Satchitānanda—our ability to live a life of meaningful service.

When we combine *sat*, *chit*, and *ānanda*, we achieve what some nondual tantric practitioners say is the highest goal of yoga: *satchitānanda*. This term means the awakening to our own personal truth, our full potential, em-

---

396. *Meditation for the Love of It*, at 42–45.

397. *Meditation for the Love of It*, at 42–43.

398. *The Splendor of Recognition*, at 32–33.

bracing it, and then experiencing the joy of offering that potential in service of something greater than ourselves.[399] As we've discussed in Chapter 2 and throughout this book, this process of discovering our unique potential and utilizing it in service to others has been referred to as the "good life," a life filled with wellbeing.[400]

Śrī—our nature for generosity and to view the world with abundance.

Another part of our highest nature is to be *śrī* (also *"shri"*), auspiciousness, to manifest wellbeing.[401] *Śrī* is the power of abundance.[402] When we choose to view the world as abundant, we see it and everyone expansively, full of possibility. Rather than view life from the perspective of scarcity, wanting to hold on to what is "mine," we instead become more generous, looking for ways to help expand wellbeing in the world, rather than hoard it. We support efforts that help others cultivate their potential, knowing that this not only makes their world brighter, but it brightens our lives as well because we live in that same world. When we act out of abundance, we spread "good fortune everywhere."[403] When we pursue meaning in our lives as a way of increasing our own wellbeing, we learn to look for opportunities that give others a chance to also be more meaningful members of society.

Śrī is also the power of beauty, grace, sacredness, nobility, and dignity.[404] We can choose to live as a graceful, noble, and dignified person if we wish. And these are precisely the types of character traits we must develop

---

399. *Finding the Midline*, at 72–75 (discussing *satchitānanda* in terms of finding our particular strengths and then offering them in service; *citing Exquisite Love*, at 90).

400. *Flourish*, at 17–21; *see also Authentic Happiness*. New York, NY: Free Press, at 260.

401. *Auspicious Wisdom*, at 64, 70, 81 (stating that *śrī* means "life-giving," increasing "prosperity," "well-being," and "power").

402. *Enthusiasm*, at 10.

403. *Enthusiasm*, at 10–11.

404. Swami Chidvilasananda (2006). *Sadhana of the Heart*. South Fallsburg, NY: SYDA Foundation, at 38; *see also Enthusiasm*, at 10 (*Śrī* "is filled with auspiciousness, beauty, sacredness, abundance, nobility, dignity, and good fortune").

if we wish to attract into our lives positive emotion, engagement, meaning, accomplishment, and nurturing relationships. People want to spend time with us when we carry ourselves this way. However, even more than simply enriching our own lives, when we live this way, we inspire others with our example. We create an environment richer in each of these qualities. We foster a greater sense of abundance around us when others believe we are invested in their success and wellbeing.[405] The world truly becomes brighter.

Svātantrya—our power of choice.

Another of our highest qualities is *svātantrya*, freedom of choice, autonomy, the power of complete freedom to create whatever we choose.[406] We have the ability to use our potential to create our world in any way we wish, one choice at a time and one action at a time. We can choose how we think, how we view each other, and how we view ourselves. We can choose thoughts and actions that increase elements of wellbeing or, alternatively, lessen our experience of them. We are free to live as an expression of our highest nature; i.e., kind and generous, or choose not to do so. However, by remembering that life satisfaction includes living a life of meaning, in warm, nurturing companionship, with others, it becomes easier to choose attitudes such as kindness and generosity that enhance these elements of wellbeing.

Spanda—our ability to constantly increase wellbeing.

Another attribute of our highest nature is *spanda*. *Spanda* means "pulsation" or "vibration" and refers to the pulsation by which *Paramśiva* creates

---

405. *Sadhana of the Heart*, at 38–40 (stating that we can transform our world into greater abundance by ourselves living as "a beacon of light" living with an attitude of abundance, *Śri*).

406. For a discussion of *Paramśiva*'s freedom of choice, *see Triadic Heart of Śiva*, at 50; 82; *see also The Splendor of Recognition*, at 35. *Paramśiva* is not compelled to do anything. This power of free will is called *Svātantrya-śakti*, as pure Consciousness freely "projects her light" in countless diverse forms through the ongoing act of creation; *The Splendor of Recognition*, at 41.

the world.[407] This is the creative interaction between *Śiva* and *Śakti* I discussed above, the universal rhythm or "dance" responsible for all creative activity in the world.[408] As human beings, we are constantly engaged in a dance of creation ourselves, choosing with each experience whether or not to enhance wellbeing, ours as well as that of others. The interaction with others I've discussed throughout this book is a classic example of this creative dance, the vibratory energy of *spanda*, as we reflect back to another their potential and help them to express it.

Pūrnatva—our sense of completeness.

The final attribute of our highest nature I want to mention is *pūrnatva*, a sense of contentment, fullness or feeling complete.[409] In the metaphysical model, *Śiva* and *Śakti* create the world out of the sheer joy of doing so, and not to satisfy any particular desire for anything other than the joy of creating.[410] They enjoy expressing their potential. Each creation, for them, is a perfect expression of the creative joy that spawned it, no refinements necessary. This can be the case for us as well. **When we create a life that is a full expression of our highest potential, we too are full, complete. We've recognized and manifested what we have to give, without holding back. With this sense of contentment, we have no reason to harbor feelings of envy, jealousy, lack of worth, or other such emotions because we know we have offered our best.**

These personal attributes, this description of our highest nature, is just one of many important ways yoga philosophy can connect us to our full potential as human beings. It is our choice as to whether we embrace these attributes and, by doing so, express the magnificence we are each capable of being.

---

407. *The Splendor of Recognition*, at 42.

408. *The Doctrine of Vibration*, at 20–21.

409. Mishra, Kamalakar (1993). *Kashmir Saivism*. Portland, OR: Rudra Press, at 124.

410. *Kashmir Saivism*, at 124.

More effective connection with others.

Yoga is literally the "connective power" that brings together our inner self with the world, asking us to express that power in ways that will serve our "collective value for civilization."[411] Yoga philosophy offers valuable lessons on how to express ourselves in ways that create greater harmony in our relationships in the world. As an example, I want to again refer to *Patañjali's Yoga Sūtras*. We've already briefly discussed Patañjali's eight limbs and certain ways in which the *Yoga Sūtras* address meditation practices. Let's now briefly discuss Patañjali's work in terms of how it can assist us in more harmonious connection.

It appears that Patañjali did not intend that his *Yoga Sūtras* serve as a template for increasing artful engagement in the world. Historically, the goal of Patañjali's yoga was to liberate the individual from the world in order to realize the soul, a very "self-centered or egoistic" pursuit.[412] However, some commentators tell us that this goal of liberating oneself from the world can't be reached without a "moral means of interacting with others" and can "never be obtained through immoral means."[413] Imagine trying to withdraw from the distractions of the world to catch a glimpse of your divine soul when you are running from bill collectors, the police, and others angry with you for whatever reason. Obviously, some basic rules of behavior are necessary for everyone, if, for no other reason, to be left alone to meditate, free of pesky worldly pressures.

Fortunately, Patañjali provided rules for behavior that have stood the test of time. In *Yoga Sūtra* 1.33 **Patañjali advised that in order to live with a clear mind, we must learn to temper our attitudes towards others, "cultivating an attitude of friendship towards those who are happy, compassion towards those in distress, joy toward those who are**

411. Brooks, Dr. Douglas (2008). *Poised for Grace*. The Woodlands, TX: Anusara Press, at 29.

412. *The Yoga Sūtras of Patañjali*, at 252.

413. *The Yoga Sūtras of Patañjali*, at 252; *see also* Remski, Matthew (2012). *Threads of Yoga*. Toronto, Canada: Matthew Remski, at 111 (commenting on *Patañjali's Yoga Sūtras* as a work that can be utilized to create more kindness and connection in the world, shifting away from the goal of building "internal equanimity" to an "exploration of empathy as a path to self-and-other growth").

virtuous, and equanimity towards those who are nonvirtuous."[414] These attitudes "keep the mind in a state of well-being."[415] Feeling pleasure for another's happiness frees us from the negative energy associated with envy and jealousy.[416] Rather than resenting another's good fortune, we instead resonate with their joy. By feeling compassion towards those who are suffering, we become more compassionate ourselves, bolstering our own capacity to express our highest nature as a kind, benevolent, empathetic person.[417] With that type of mindset any predisposition we might have towards wishing or even inflicting harm on others is diminished.[418] Similarly, when we feel joy towards those who are virtuous, our minds open to being inspired by such behavior. We appreciate the virtuous behavior as a model for how we can behave.[419] And, by feeling equanimity towards the nonvirtuous we avoid the mental turmoil associated with judging others. We don't fill ourselves with anger, hatred, and disdain. Instead, we cultivate a relaxed, peaceful mind, keeping our boundaries with such a person. Free of the distracting and unnecessary mental and emotional energy we might otherwise spend keeping fresh our ill-will towards someone, we are better able to identify and embrace opportunities for building wellbeing.[420]

Developing these attitudes is an essential practice that "spills over into all aspects of life's affairs and social interactions."[421] As we seek to develop not only greater self-awareness, but also more effective connection with others, these attitudes help us become the type of person to whom others are drawn. Our minds remain clear, able to quickly and effectively iden-

---

414. *The Yoga Sūtras of Patañjali*, at 128 (translating Patañjali's *Yoga Sūtra* 1.33)

415. *Light on the Yoga Sūtras of Patañjali*, at 86.

416. *The Yoga Sūtras of Patañjali*, at 129.

417. Satchidananda, Swami (2003 ed). *The Yoga Sūtras of Patañjali*. Yogaville, VA: Integral Yoga Publications, at 55 (discussing *Yoga Sūtra* 1.33). When referring to this resource, I will add "(Satchidananda)" to distinguish it from other books of the same name.

418. *The Yoga Sūtras of Patañjali*, at 129.

419. *The Yoga Sūtras of Patañjali* (Satchidananda), at 55–56.

420. *The Yoga Sūtras of Patañjali*, at 129–130.

421. *The Yoga Sūtras of Patañjali*, at 130 (stating that the mindfulness taught by this *Sūtra* is consistent with the goal of engaging in "benevolent social action in the world").

tify opportunities to experience positive emotion, engage in meaningful activities, accomplish worthwhile goals, and build nurturing relationships.

In addition, Patañjali gave us the rules for behavior contained in the five *yamas* we briefly discussed in Chapter 9.[422] The *yamas*, the first of the eight limbs of Patañjali's yoga, are rules for treating others. They provide a moral means for how to behave in the world.[423] Listed at *Yoga Sūtra* 2.30 and discussed in *Yoga Sūtras* 2.31 and 2.33 to 2.39, they are: nonviolence (*ahiṁsā*); truthfulness (*satya*); abstention from stealing (*asteya*); sexual integrity (*brahmacarya*); and renunciation of unnecessary possessions (*aparagraha*).[424]

Following is a very brief overview of each of these five *yamas*. Again, it isn't my purpose in this book to provide a detailed commentary about Patañjali, or any of the other points of yoga philosophy I discuss. Rather, my objective is to bring certain of these ideas, as well as resources, to your attention, opening the door for you to consider how you might use this information to enhance your wellbeing.

Ahiṁsā.

According to the commentators, *ahiṁsā*, or non-violence, is the root of all five of the *yamas*, with the goal of each yamas being to avoid causing harm.[425] *Ahiṁsā* goes far beyond the avoidance of deliberately injuring somebody physically. There are many ways to harm another. For example, we can harm another with our words, as when we speak to somebody without regard for their basic dignity or feelings. Another way we can harm

---

422. Each of Patañjali's *Yoga Sūtras* can be read to pertain to information useful for increasing our wellbeing.

423. *The Yoga Sūtras of Patañjali*, at 252.

424. *The Yoga Sūtras of Patañjali*, at 242–243; *Light on the Yoga Sūtras of Patañjali*, at 142–143. For an excellent discussion of the *yamas* and *niyamas* as they apply in everyday life, consider Adele, Deborah (2009). *The Yamas and Niyamas*. Duluth, MN: On-Word Bound Books, and Main, Darren (2014 ed.) *Yoga and the Path of the Urban Mystic*. San Francisco, CA: Surya Rising Books.

425. *The Yoga Sūtras of Patañjali*, at 243 (citing the commentator Vyasa).

another is by spreading gossip. This is harmful, even if it is fact-based, because it damages that person's reputation and potentially impacts, in a chain of cause and effect, many others who interact with that person; i.e., their children, their partners, their relatives, etc. While sometimes we do need to talk about another person when they aren't around, for example, to protect others from that person, those occasions are really quite rare in comparison to the times we needlessly cast somebody in a negative light in conversations when that person isn't around to defend themselves. Another example we might not otherwise consider as harmful is a failure to act in certain circumstances. Sometimes staying silent or not intervening in a situation will result in harm to others. Consider, again, the subject of gossip. By remaining silent we contribute to whatever cause and effect that gossip session will put into action.

Non-harming starts with our attitude towards ourselves. **Non-harming "should be the gateway to our thoughts, words, and behavior."**[426] We learn to watch that we don't cause harm to ourselves by harboring self-defeating thoughts and emotions. We exacerbate that harm to ourselves by then putting our negative views of ourselves into words; "I'm so dumb" being a classic example. Also, how often do we speak ill of others purely to be self-indulgent? All we're doing in that case is feeding our own negative thoughts and emotions, harming our own path to greater wellbeing. Are we gossiping because we're jealous? Angry? *Ahiṁsā* asks us to turn our attention inside and figure out what is driving such feelings and words. We learn to immediately spot and examine any negative thought about ourselves that might arise. We stop vocalizing such thoughts. We develop the skills of emotional resiliency so that we don't allow our emotions to prompt us into thoughts and actions that bring harm to ourselves or to others.

Satya.

Satya, truthfulness, involves more than just telling the truth. We make sure we know what we are talking about, that we are not basing what we say on false assumptions or incomplete knowledge of the facts. We need to

426. *Finding the Midline*, at 261–262.

ask: is this true? Do I know if I'm stating facts or, instead, spreading what might be an inaccurate rumor or supposition?

Even if we know what we are about to say is true, we still have to consider whether we might cause unnecessary harm by saying it. In such cases we ask ourselves why we are passing this information on to another, knowing it likely will cause somebody harm. Is what we are about to say really necessary? Does the information truly add value to the world in some way? For example, if the information is needed to safeguard others, then we have a moral obligation to help. Does it help create harmony or does it needlessly injure another?[427] Even if what we wish to say is true and necessary, are we saying it in the kindest way we can; "one should not tell the truth unkindly."[428]

Asteya.

Patañjali lists *asteya*, non-stealing, as the third of his five *yamas*, or moral restraints. This refers in part to the literal interpretation of stealing, as in taking another's property. Hopefully, we all know not to take a person's wallet or physical property. But this *Sūtra* asks much more of us. We violate this rule when we needlessly injure another's reputation, dignity, or potential to enjoy wellbeing. We "steal" when we take credit for somebody else's ideas or work product.

When we are rude to another, we steal some of their self-esteem. We steal when we discriminate against people of other races, cultures, a different gender, or for some other distinction, for no reason other than the fact that they belong to such groups. We are robbing them of the same opportunity we wish for ourselves and our family, a chance to work hard, carve out a decent life, and live with dignity. When we take that opportunity away for discriminatory reasons, we steal their opportunity to thrive. Also, keeping the cardinal rule of *ahimsā* in mind, when we deny others a

427. *The Yoga Sūtras of Patañjali*, at 245 (discussing the purpose of speech to be "transferal of one's knowledge to others and should not be deceitful, misleading, or devoid of value").

428. *The Yoga Sūtras of Patañjali*, at 246.

fair opportunity in such a way, we do violence to harmony in our community and to the possibility of a more abundant world. We steal the value of their potential, left unrealized because of us. Thus, we are doing violence to ourselves because we live in that same world and that world will be a bit dimmer, a bit less, as a result. We also do violence to ourselves because such discriminatory views and actions can only live in a mind that views life through a lens of scarcity, rather than abundance.

Brahmacarya.

Patañjali's fourth *yama* is *brahmacarya*, which translates as celibacy. While Patañjali likely meant just that, the *Sūtra* today often is interpreted to mean sexual restraint and integrity, the avoidance of "sexual immorality."[429] When we pursue sexual relations, there are always ramifications, including feelings to consider. This is particularly true in situations where there is a power differential, such as in the workplace. Before putting people's feelings, such as self-respect, as well as job security, comfort, and opportunities to thrive, in harm's way, we have to consider the consequences. In a power differential at work, for example, even a fully consensual relationship creates the potential for harm down the road to the career of the participant in the less powerful position. Yoga demands of us that we consider all such issues and avoid harm.

Aparagraha.

The fifth *yama* is *aparagraha*, renunciation of unnecessary possessions, including hoarding, holding on to more material possessions than we need. This *Sūtra* is a caution to us to restrain our consumer habits, using only the resources we truly require.[430] For example, we must consider the stress we place on our planet when we consume without thought to the impact of

---

429. *Light on the Yoga Sūtras of Patañjali*, at 151 (relating *brahmacarya* to the the vow of nonviolence, *ahimsā*, the root of all five yamas.)

430. *Threads of Yoga*, at 109–110.

our consumption. The *Sūtra* asks us to make political choices that might, depending on our circumstances, require slightly greater sacrifice through taxes so that others have a fair chance to develop their potential. I think back to our Vermont town meeting where, each year, citizens of our town, many of whom need to watch their budgets closely, vote every year to give some tax dollars to various organizations that help others, even when they themselves are not part of the groups that will be helped. We are challenged to ask how much we really need when our increasing comfort takes opportunity away from someone else.

In summary, the *yamas* give us a context for "understanding the impact that our choices and behavior may have on others."[431] This context allows us to behave in a way that creates harmony with others and also as the best version of ourselves as a human being. We commit to behaving in a way that is caring and honest. In doing so we become a person with whom others desire to connect.[432] By taking time to more thoroughly know ourselves and by following a set of rules for how to treat others, we maximize our ability to achieve the highest level of personal wellbeing.

---

431. *The Art of Vinyasa*, at 36.

432. *The Art of Vinyasa*, at 36.

Additional resources.

There is so much more I could say about yoga philosophy and how it offers us wonderful lessons of how to better connect with ourselves and with others.[433] However, that is for another day.[434] This chapter has of course been only a very brief glimpse of what yoga philosophy offers by way of guiding us to the highest expression of ourselves and showing how to create harmony in our relationships. If you develop sufficient awareness and focus, and then choose to live fully as a kind, generous person who sees the world as abundant—wellbeing will find you.

---

433. For further exploration into the breadth of yoga philosophy, consider two books mentioned previously: *The Yoga Tradition* and *Yoga Immorality and Freedom*. Also consider Keller, Doug. *Heart of the Yogi*, South Riding, VA: Doug Keller. And a necessary resource is the short but beautiful *Bhagavad Gita*, "the Song of the Blessed One." *Poised for Grace*, at 3. Considered perhaps the most "beloved scripture of India," the *Bhagavad Gita* constitutes the "essence" of yoga philosophy. Yogananda, Paramahansa (1999 ed). *The Bhagavad Gita*. Los Angeles, CA: The Self-Realization Fellowship, at xvii. *See also*, Feuerstein, Dr. Georg (2011). *The Bhagavad Gita*. Boston, MA: Shambhala Publications, Inc., at 58–59 (referring to the *Bhagavad Gita* as "the most popular religio-spiritual scripture of Hinduism" and the "essence" of earlier teachings); *and see*, *Poised for Grace*, at 17–18 ("If it were possible to summarize the *Bhagavadgita*'s teachings, then it would be encapsulated in the word 'yoga,'" which ultimately refers to "connection—its presence or absence, its success or failure, and the far reach of such effects into every feature of human life"). *Poised for Grace* provides a discussion of the *Bhagavad Gita* from a nondual tantric perspective. I consider *Poised for Grace* to be an essential resource for building my own life of wellbeing and strongly recommend having it in hand as you read through whatever commentary of the *Bhagavad Gita* you select.

434. This book is the first in a series.

Conclusion

I've shared with you a theory of wellbeing as well as a pathway for how to build a life of wellbeing for yourself. To understand each element of wellbeing you not only have this book as your go-to manual, you also have access, through the footnotes, to answers for questions that might arise along your path.

My hope is that this book will help when you find that, despite your best intentions, old patterns of thought and behavior begin disrupting you on your quest for wellbeing. Some therapists call these patterns our "old tapes," and they often show up seemingly out of nowhere, at just the precise moment when an opportunity to build wellbeing presents itself, promptly causing us to sabotage that opportunity. It took me quite a bit of time and more than a little heartbreaking disappointment before I figured out that no matter what I knew about creating a life of wellbeing, it didn't matter if I let my anger, fears, and self-doubts hijack me. I mentioned these patterns, the old tapes, throughout this book and discussed the value of building emotional resilience to get control over them. I've offered suggestions for regaining that control, as well as plenty of information in the footnotes to help you put yourself in charge of whatever psychological varmints reside in your mind.

And in Part 2 I told you about yoga, the means to pull together all the information in this manual. Regardless of what we know about wellbeing and emotional resilience, we won't get too far unless we develop some mastery over our thoughts. We require a clear mind in order to recognize and then evaluate options, to take advantage of the innumerable opportunities life offers us to experience positive emotion, engagement, and personal relationships, or to create meaning and accomplishment. As part of that process we must learn how to sustain a focus on whatever choices we make in order to see them through successfully. Yoga is perhaps uniquely suited to teach us those skills.

Finally, I've provided information about better knowing yourself as well as more effectively connecting with others. So much of wellbeing, as we've learned, involves positive, warm connections with others. To that end I've shared with you just a taste of what yoga philosophy teaches us about our highest potential, our ability to be kind, generous, and curious about others. These are the types of traits that draw people to us, increasing the presence of warm, nurturing relationships in our life.

There is so much more to what yoga offers us in terms of refining our own personal route to wellbeing. I've only touched on that value. In the future, I'll share more of yoga with you in books that build on the foundation we've built in this book.

Bibliography

Abhinavagupta (2004 ed). *Gitartha Samgraha. Abhinavagupta's Commentary on the Bhagavad Gita* (B. Marjanovic, Trans.). New Delhi, India: First Impression.

Adele, Deborah (2009). *The Yamas and Niyamas.* Duluth, MN: On-Word Bound Books.

Blackburn, Dr. Elizabeth and Epel, Dr. Elissa (2018). *The Telomere Effect.* New York, NY: Grand Central Publishing.

Brooks, Dr. Douglas (1992). *Auspicious Wisdom.* Albany, NY: State University of New York, Albany.

Brooks, Dr. Douglas (2008). *Poised for Grace.* The Woodlands, TX: Anusara Press.

Bryant, Dr. Edwin (2009). *The Yoga Sūtras of Patañjali.* New York, NY: North Point Press.

Bryant, Dr. Fred and Veroff, Dr. Joseph (2007). *Savoring: A New Model of Positive Experience.* Mahwah, NJ: Lawrence Erlbaum Associates, Inc.

Carrera, Rev. Jaganath (2015, 5th ed). *Inside the Yoga Sūtras.* Buckingham, VA: Integral Yoga Publications.

Chidvilasananda, Swami (1996). *The Yoga of Discipline.* South Fallsburg, NY: SYDA Foundation.

Chidvilasananda, Swami (1997). *Enthusiasm.* South Fallsburg, NY: SYDA Foundation

Chidvilasananda, Swami (2006). *Sadhana of the Heart.* South Fallsburg, NY: SYDA Foundation.

Cope, Stephen (2012). *The Great Work of Your Life: A Guide for the Journey to Your True Calling.* New York, NY: Bantam Books.

Covey, Stephen R. (2013 ed). *The 7 Habits of Highly Effective People.* New York, NY: Simon & Schuster.

Csikszentmihalyi, Dr. Mihaly (2008 ed.). *Flow: The Psychology of Optimal Experience.* New York, NY: HarperCollins Publishers.

Csikszentmihalyi, Dr. Mihaly (2013 ed). *Creativity.* New York, NY: HarperCollins Publishers.

Cyrulnik, Dr. Boris (2011 ed.) *Resilience.* London, ENG: The Penguin Group.

Dalai Lama (2002). *How to Practice: The Way to a Meaningful Life.* New York, NY: Pocket Books.

Desikachar, T.K.V. (1995). *The Heart of Yoga.* Rochester, VT: Inner Traditions International.

Doniger, Dr. Wendy (1991). *The Rig Veda.* New York, NY: Penguin Group.

Dorigan, William (2013). *Finding the Midline.* Winter Park, CO: LuHen Publications, LLC.

Duckworth, Dr. Angela (2016). *Grit.* New York, NY: Scribner.

Duhigg, Charles (2014 ed). *The Power of Habit.* New York, NY: Random House.

Dyczkowski, Dr. Mark (1987). *The Doctrine of Vibration.* Albany, NY: State University of New York Press.

Eliade, Mircea (2009 ed.) *Yoga Immortality and Freedom.* Princeton, NJ: Princeton University Press.

Festinger, Leon (1962 ed). *A Theory of Cognitive Dissonance.* Stanford, CA: Stanford University Press.

Feuerstein, Dr. Georg (1998). *Tantra The Path of Ecstasy.* Boston, MA: Shambhala Publications, Inc.

Feuerstein, Dr. Georg (2001 ed). *The Yoga Tradition.* Prescott, AZ: Hohm Press.

Feuerstein, Dr. Georg (2007). *Yoga Morality*. Prescott, AZ: Hohm Press.

Feuerstein, Dr. Georg (2011). *The Bhagavad Gita*. Boston, MA: Shambhala Publications, Inc.

Fontana, Dr. David (2002 ed). *The Meditator's Handbook*. London, ENG: Thorsons.

Frankl, Dr. Viktor (2006 ed). *Man's Search for Meaning*. Boston, MA: Beacon Press.

Fredrickson, Dr. Barbara (2009). *Positivity*. New York, NY: Three Rivers Press.

Fredrickson, Dr. Barbara (2014 ed). *Love 2.0*. New York, NY: Penguin Group (USA) LLC.

Freeman, Richard (2010. *The Mirror of Yoga*. Boston, MA: Shambhala Publications, Inc.

Freeman, Richard and Taylor, Mary (2016). *The Art of Vinyasa*. Boulder, CO: Shambhala Publications, Inc.

Frenette, David (2017 ed). *The Path of Centering Prayer*. Boulder, CO: Sounds True.

Fritz, Robert (1989 ed.) *The Path of Least Resistance. Learning to Become the Creative Force in your Own Life*. New York, NY: Ballantine Books.

Genco, Mark (2017). *Inner Jiu Jitsu*. Denver, CO: Mark Genco.

Goleman, Dr. Daniel (2006). *Social Intelligence*. New York, NY: Bantam Dell.

Goleman, Dr. Daniel (2013). *Focus*. New York, NY: HarperCollins.

Goleman, Dr. Daniel and Davidson, Dr. Richard J. (2017). *Altered Traits*. New York, NY: Penguin Random House LLC.

Iyengar, B.K.S. (1979 ed). *Light on Yoga*. New York, NY: Schocken Books.

Iyengar, B.K.S. (2005). *Light on Life*. Emmaus, PA: Rodale.

Iyengar, B.K.S. (2002 ed). *The Tree of Yoga*. Boston, MA: Shambhala Publications, Inc.

Iyengar, B.K.S. (2002 ed). *Light on the Yoga Sūtras of Patañjali*. London, ENG: Thorsons

Iyengar, B.K.S. (2011 ed). *Light on Prāṇāyāma*. India: HarperCollins Publishers India.

Iyenger, B.K.S. (2012). *Core of the Yoga Sūtras*. London, ENG: HarperThorsens.

Iyengar, B.K.S. (2001). *Yoga The Path to Holistic Health*. London, England: Dorling Kindersley Limited.

Iyengar, B.K.S. (2016). "Why should we practice *prāṇāyāma?*" In (Mehta, Rajvi H. ed). *Yoga Rahasya* (Vol. 23, No.1), Mumbai, Yog.

Iyengar, Getta (1990). *Yoga A Gem for Women*. Spokane, WA: Timeless Books.

Keating, Thomas (2009 ed.). *Intimacy with God: An Introduction to Centering Prayer*. New York, NY: The Crossroads Publishing Company.

Keller, Doug. *Heart of the Yogi*. South Riding, VA: Doug Keller.

Kempton, Sally (2002). *Meditation for the Love of It*. Boulder, CO: Sounds True, Inc.

Mahony, Dr. William (2010). *Exquisite Love*. The Woodlands, TX: Anusara Press.

Main, Darren (2014 ed.) *Yoga and the Path of the Urban Mystic*. San Francisco, CA: Surya Rising Books.

Maslow, Dr. Abraham H (1970 ed). *Motivation and Personality*. New York, NY: Harper & Row, Publishers, Inc.

Maslow, Dr. Abraham H. (1971). *The Farther Reaches of Human Nature*. New York, NY: Penguin Books.

May, Dr. Rollo (1953). *Man's Search for Himself*. New York, NY: Dell Publishing.

May, Dr. Rollo (1975). *The Courage to Create*. New York, NY: W.W. Norton & Company, Inc.

May, Dr. Rollo (1983). *The Discovery of Being*. New York, NY: W.W. Norton & Company, Inc.

Merton, Thomas (1996 ed). *Contemplative Prayer*. New York, NY: Image.

Mishra, Kamalakar (1993). *Kashmir Saivism*. Portland, OR: Rudra Press

Muktibodhananda, Swami (2008 ed). *Haṭha Yoga Pradīpikā*. Mungar, Bihar, INDIA: Bihar School of Yoga.

Ortega, Dr. Paul-Muller (1989). *The Triadic Heart of Śiva*. Albany, NY: State University of New York Press, Albany.

Peterson, Dr. Christopher and Seligman, Dr. Martin (2004). *Character Strengths and Virtues: A Handbook and Classification*. New York, NY: Oxford University Press, Inc.

Reivich, Dr. Karen and Shatte, Dr. Andrew (2002). *The Reslience Factor, 7 Keys To Finding Your Inner Strengths and Overcoming Life's Hurdles*. New York, NY: Three Rivers Press.

Remski, Matthew (2012). *Threads of Yoga*. Toronto, Canada.

Ruiz, Don Miquel (1997). *The Four Agreements*. San Rafael, CA: Amber-Allen Publishing.

Salzberg, Sharon (2011). *Real Happiness, The Power of Meditation*. New York, NY: The Workman Publishing Company, Inc.

Satchidananda, Swami (2003 ed). *The Yoga Sūtras of Patañjali*. Yogaville, VA: Integral Yoga Publications.

Seligman, Dr. Martin (2002). *Authentic Happiness*. New York, NY: Free Press.

Seligman, Dr. Martin (2006 ed.) *Learned Optimism*. New York, NY: Vintage Books.

Seligman, Dr. Martin (2011). *Flourish*. New York, NY: The Free Press.

Shantananda, Swami. *The Spender of Recognition*. South Fallsburg, NY: SYDA Foundation.

Siegel, Dr. Daniel J. (2007). *The Mindful Brain*. New York, NY: W.W. Norton & Company, Inc.

Siegel, Dr. Daniel (2011 ed). *Mindsight*. New York, NY: Bantam Books.

Siegel, Dr. Daniel J. (2018). *Aware*. New York, NY: Penguin Random House.

Sood, Dr. Amit (2015). *The Mayo Clinic Handbook for Happiness*. Boston, MA: Da Capo Press.

Tolle. Ekhart (2005). *A New Earth: Awakening to Your Life's Purpose*. New York, NY: Penguin Group.

Vaillant, Dr. George E. (2012). *Triumphs of Experience*. Cambridge, MA: The Belknap Press of Harvard University Press.

White, Dr. David Gordon (2000). *Tantra In Practice*. Princeton, NJ: Princeton University Press.

White, Dr. David Gordon (2007 ed.). *The Alchemical Body*. Chicago, IL: The University of Chicago.

Yogananda, Paramahansa (1999 ed.). *The Bhagavad Gita*. Los Angeles, CA: The Self-Realization Fellowship.

Acknowledgements

It is truly impossible to thank, by name, everyone who contributed to this book in one fashion or another—perhaps through their lectures, their own writing, in conversation, or even by something they said or did that inspired me. So, I offer a general thank you to the many people—teacher, student, friend, and stranger—who served as a catalyst for an idea that made its way into this book.

Dr. Martin Seligman's work in positive psychology has been an important guide in my own life and without which I wouldn't have the well-being theory I've shared with you in this book. Similarly, I want to thank the many individuals whose work I've referenced either in the text or in footnotes. Their dedication and work in the fields of behavior and wellbeing provide a wealth of information available to help us build wellbeing, relationships, and emotional resilience in our lives.

Work by B.K.S. Iyengar, Richard Freeman, Georg Feuerstein, Dr. Douglas Brooks, Dr. Paul Muller-Ortega, and many others, provide key insight on how yoga is such a uniquely invaluable means for building wellbeing, including its value for teaching us the all-important skills of awareness, focus, and the ability to more effectively connect with ourselves and others.

Several people provided guidance through the various stages of this book. Dr. Thomas Storer provided critical feedback in the early draft stage, helping me to find my voice. He also offered assistance later on a number of ideas. Next, as he has done for a number of years, Joe Soma helped me to make this book the best expression of me I could make it. Certified Iyengar teacher Craig Kurtz offered important feedback that greatly enhanced the substance of my discussion of why yoga is such an invaluable practice. Laura Smyth, of Smythtype Design wore so many hats in terms of her assistance—discussion of concepts, organization, presentation, and encouragement, as well as design, formatting, and production expertise. I want to express my gratitude to Laura for all that plus the handholding—she really does pick up her phone when I call and, on way more than one occasion, offer much needed encouragement.

I owe a debt of gratitude to my neighbor, Jeff Koonz, who has not only supported me but also pestered me to make sure that the book kept moving forward. In addition, his volunteer work is an ongoing inspiration to me as an example of how a person can live the life of meaning Dr. Viktor Frankl asks of us—to pay attention to what life is asking of us each day.

My family is the greatest resource for not only support but also inspiration. My son Jeff has, on many occasions, served as a sounding board for the discussion of thoughts about both substance and approach. Plus, my desire to have a warm connection with he and his family was a prime motivation for me to undertake the pursuit of wellbeing to begin with. Without my desire for that connection, I probably wouldn't have been reading Martin Seligman and his peers and, thus, wouldn't have written about what I learned.

Index

Note: Footnote information is indicated by n and note number following the page number.

About the Author

BILL DORIGAN is a certified yoga teacher, lecturer, a retired trial attorney, and a published author in the legal field. Following a career as an equity partner in one of the nation's leading law firms, Bill completed a master's degree studying the correlation of yoga philosophy with behavioral psychology. Following completion of that degree Bill combined his extensive experience litigating high profile lawsuits with his deep understanding of yoga philosophy to write the 2013 book, *Finding the Midline—How yoga helps a trial lawyer make friends and connect to Spirit*. Following publication of that book Bill continued his research in behavioral psychology, focusing on how the practice and study of yoga provides a means for optimizing wellbeing. As a result, he created this book, *A Manual for Wellbeing, Book One—Using Yoga to Enrich Your Life*. In his spare time Bill continues his practice in martial arts (he has been awarded three black belts), regularly practices and teaches yoga and its philosophy, and enjoys the beauty of the Green Mountains of Vermont, his home.

COMING SOON

Book Two further explores the creation mythology of nondual tantric yoga as a source of theories and practices for further cultivating our own highest nature, becoming increasingly skilled at living a life rich in meaning and connection with others—a life of abundant, even self-transcendent, wellbeing.

Manufactured by Amazon.ca
Bolton, ON

33410874R00103